Step by Step Guide to Learn English
52 Topics for 52 Weeks of the Year

Practice Book
for English Learners

All rights reserved

Teachers are allowed to make copies of the Question-and-Answer pages, limited for personal use in their own classrooms, not exceeding 200 pages. For bulk use by a school or education department, written permission must be obtained from the author or his authorized agent.

Apart from said educational non-profit use, no part of this publication may be reproduced, stored or transmitted in any form or by any means, electronic, mechanical, photocopying, recording, scanning, or otherwise without written permission from the publisher. It is illegal to copy this book, post it to a website, or distribute it by any other means without permission.

Copyright © 2022

Introduction

Hi,

This book is meant for English teachers and learners alike. If you are an English teacher, you can photocopy pages from this book and hand them out to students to practice these questions with one another.

If you are an English learner, you can go over these questions and read the sample answers. Ideally you should try and practice these with a partner to improve your fluency.

I hope these questions help you in your classes when you are a teacher, and with your English if you are trying to improve your English ability.

Contents

1. About You
2. Daily Routines
3. How often/ How many?
4. Have you ever?
5. Do you ever?
6. Holidays
7. Weather
8. Shopping
9. Movies
10. Television
11. Fashion
12. Emotions
13. Health
14. Music
15. Hobbies
16. Crime
17. Dating

18. Favorites
19. Travel
20. Would you rather?
21. Time
22. Books
23. Sports
24. Religion
25. News
26. Money
27. Parties
28. Goals
29. Technology
30. Problems
31. Accidents
32. Work and Jobs
33. Love
34. Food
35. First Time
36. If you could

37. Culture
38. Wishes
39. Gossip
40. Birthday
41. Advice
42. Environment
43. Family
44. Social Media
45. Animals
46. Learning English
47. Last Time
48. How do you?
49. What if?
50. Social Issues
51. Personality
52. Job Interview

1 About You

QUESTIONS & ANSWERS (Q&A) STUDENT A

1. **What's your name?** My name is Giorgio.
2. **Who is your best friend? How did you meet?** My best friend is Billy. We met at middle school.
3. **What's your email address?** My email address is giorgio@gmail.com.
4. **Do you have any siblings?** I have three siblings – two brothers and a sister.
5. **What kind of music do you like?** I like rock music but I don't like metal.
6. **How often do you eat out? What's your favorite restaurant?** I eat out about two times (twice) a week. My favorite restaurant is McDonald's.
7. **What do you like to do on your birthday?** I like to go to amusement parks and ride rollercoasters.
8. **Where did you grow up?** Describe the place. I grew up in a small town and my house was near my school.
9. **Who is your favorite family member?** My favorite family member is my brother because he is funny and we play games together.
10. **What sports do you like?** I like watching football. I also enjoy playing basketball.

Q&A - 1 ABOUT YOU - STUDENT B

1. **What's your last name?** (Surname / family name) My last name is Smith.
2. **What's your phone number?** My phone number 011 555 7789.
3. **What do you usually do on weekends?** I usually meet my friends at the park.
4. **What's your favorite snack?** My favorite snack is dried fruit.
5. **When is your birthday? How old are you?** My birthday is March 18th. I am 20 years old.

6. **What is your best skill?** I am good at playing tennis.
7. **Do you have a pet? / Would you like a pet?** Yes, I have a dog. His name is Biscuit.
8. **What's your job? / What's your parent's job? / What do you do?** I'm a teacher. I work at a school.
9. **What hobbies do you have?** What do you do in your free time? I like to exercise in my free time.
10. **What app do you use the most on your phone?** I often use Instagram to look at my friends' photos.

2 Daily Routines

QUESTIONS & ANSWERS STUDENT A

1. **What time do you usually wake up?** I usually wake up at 8am.
2. **Do you have a busy schedule?** Yes, I am busy during the week but I rest on weekends.
3. **Which do you like better: Mornings or afternoons?** I prefer mornings over afternoons because I like eating breakfast.
4. **What do you usually do on weekday mornings?** On weekday mornings I go to school.
5. **Where do you like to hang out during your free time?** When I have time available, I like to go for a walk around the park near my home.
6. **Do you like to exercise? Why/Why not?** Yes, I like to exercise because it gives me more energy and makes me feel good. /I don't like to exercise; I prefer relaxing at home.
7. **What is something you waste a lot of time on?** I waste a lot of time playing on my phone or watching TV.
8. **Can you tell me about what you like to read?** I like to read articles on the internet about my hobbies.
9. **Can you cook? How often do you make dinner?** Yes, I can cook. I cook dinner four times a week. /No, I can't cook very well. I never make dinner; my mom prepares dinner for my family.
10. **How do you relax before going to bed?** I relax by playing a game or checking Instagram on my phone before going to bed.

Q&A 2 - DAILY ROUTINES - STUDENT B

1. **What time do you go to bed?** I go to sleep very late, usually around 11 pm.
2. **Are you usually early, on time, or late?** Sometimes I arrive late to appointments. When that happens, my friends get upset with me.
3. **Do you take naps?** I love taking naps on a long bus or train journey.

- **What do you do on weekend mornings?** On weekend mornings I watch TV after waking up, then have breakfast with my family.
- **What do you like to do during your free time?** During my free time I play computer games or meet friends.
- **Where do you eat lunch? What do you usually have?** I eat lunch at the school cafeteria.
- **Can you describe a place you like to walk to?** I like to take a walk around my neighborhood in the afternoon.
- **Do you spend a lot of time online? What do you do?** I spend a lot of time on social media such as Facebook and Instagram. I also visit funny websites or play games.
- **How do you commute to school/work?** I go to school by bus.

- **How many hours of TV do you watch every day?** I rarely watch TV. It is more convenient to stream shows on Netflix or YouTube.

3 How often/ How many?

QUESTIONS & ANSWERS STUDENT A

- **How often do you watch a movie?** I watch a movie twice a month.
- **How many times do you check social media every day?** I check social media throughout the day, probably far too often.
- **How often do you eat junk food?** I eat junk food about three times a week.
- **How often do you go hiking or go for a walk?** I go hiking once every two weeks. (I go hiking twice a month.)
- **How many times a day do you brush your teeth?** I brush my teeth three times a day or after meals.
- **How often do you read? What books do you like?** I read a book a month. I especially enjoy reading adventure books.
- **How often do you dream at night?** Sometimes when I sleep, I have a dream; but when I wake up, I seldom remember it.
- **How often will you ride your bicycle this summer?** I don't have a bicycle so I hardly ever ride one.
- **How often do you get into trouble?** I rarely get into trouble at school because I always do my best and behave well.
- **How often do you travel to other cities?** I hardly ever travel to other cities unless it is for a family event.

Q&A 3 - HOW OFTEN/ HOW MANY? - STUDENT B

- **How many times do you shower every day?** I take a shower once a day, usually in the morning before school.
- **How often do you post on Facebook or Instagram?** I only post on social media when something interesting or noteworthy happens.
- **How often do you shop for new clothes?** I only go to buy new clothes when there is something I need.
- **How often do you eat dessert?** I enjoy dessert frequently, especially after dinner.

1. **How often do you study English?** I study English every day.
2. **How often do you say "I love you" to your parents?** I only say "I love you" to my parents when they give me a present.
3. **How often do you go to the dentist?** I visit the dentist once or twice a year.
4. **How often do you visit your grandparents?** My grandparents live near me so I see them a few times every week.
5. **How often do you go grocery shopping?** My mom and I go grocery shopping at least once a week.
6. **How often will you exercise in the future?** I want to exercise and be more active in the future.

4 Have you ever?

QUESTIONS & ANSWERS STUDENT A

- **Have you ever lost your wallet?** Yes, I've lost my wallet in a taxi before. It slipped out of my pocket.
- **Have you ever broken a bone?** No, I've never broken a bone. / Yes, I've broken my arm before. I was climbing a tree and fell down.
- **Have you ever gotten into a fight?** Yes, unfortunately I got into a fight at school.
- **Have you ever lied to your parents?** Yes, I told them that I was going to the library, but instead I went to the arcade.
- **Have you ever met a celebrity?** No, I've never met a celebrity. But I have seen a famous actor from far away.
- **Have you ever made food for more than 10 people?** No, I haven't made food for ten people. / Yes, I've prepared sandwiches for a party.
- Have you ever been to the emergency room at a hospital? What happened? Yes, I accidentally cut my hand while slicing tomatoes and went to the ER (emergency room) to get stitches.
- **Have you ever been to a wedding?** Yes, I went to my cousin's wedding last spring.
- **Have you ever cried during a movie?** Yes, I've cried while watching a very sad movie.
- **Have you ever fallen in love/ had a crush on someone?** I had a crush when I was in elementary school. I sent her a letter, but she rejected my affection, which made me cry.

Q&A - 4 HAVE YOU EVER? - STUDENT B

- **Have you ever done volunteering for a non-profit organization?** Yes, I have volunteered at a nursing home. I had good conversations with old people.
- **Have you ever been on TV? Would you like to be on TV?** Yes, once I was interviewed by the local news channel while I was at school. /No, but

I would like to be an actor in the future.

- **Have you ever missed your stop to get off the bus or subway?** Yes, I was on the subway and fell asleep. I woke up late and missed my stop.
- **Have you ever slept in a tent?** Yes, when I was young, I went camping with my cousins and we slept in a tent.
- **Have you ever fainted in public?** No, I've never fainted in public. / Yes, one morning last year I didn't eat breakfast and was tired. While standing outside I fainted. People rushed to help me.
- **Have you ever fired a gun?** No, I've never shot a gun. / Yes, I fired my dad's rifle once.
- **Have you ever been to a funeral?** Yes, last year my grandmother passed away. We went to her funeral to say good bye. (If someone's family member dies you can say ~ I'm sorry. You have my condolences.)
- **Have you ever ridden a horse?** Yes, I've ridden a horse. Even though it was really big and a little scary, it was a fun experience.
- **Have you ever run a race?** Yes, I've run a race and got second place!
- **Have you ever gotten a bad haircut?** Yes, last year I got a bad haircut. I was so upset with the hairdresser!

5 Do you ever?

QUESTIONS & ANSWERS STUDENT A

1. **Do you ever go to bed late?** Yes, I do. Sometimes I go to bed late because I've watched a movie.
2. **Do you ever feel jealous of your friends?** Yes, I do. When my friend receives something that I want, I feel jealous (envious). / No, I don't. I always feel happy when my friends succeed.
3. **Do you ever lie to your parents?** Yes, I lie to my parents when I don't want to get into trouble. / No, I never lie to my parents. I always tell the truth.
4. **Do you ever get angry?** Yes, sometimes I get angry when I have an argument with my brother. / No, I rarely get angry. I always try to stay calm.
5. **Do you ever wish you were someone else?** Yes, I do. I wish I was a famous celebrity or someone rich. / No, I don't. I love my life and enjoy being myself.
6. **Do you ever donate blood?** Yes, I often donate blood. My blood type is A+. / No, I never donate blood.
7. **Do you ever consider getting plastic surgery?** Yes, I do. I would like to change some parts of my face. / No, I am perfectly happy with my body as it is.
8. **Do you ever tease your brother or sister?** Yes, I do. That is why we have siblings! In order to tease them! / No, I don't. I love my brother and sister and would never tease them.
9. **Do you ever go on trips alone?** Yes, I go on trips alone. A few weeks ago, I went to another city on my own. /No, I always go on trips with friends or family.
10. **Do you ever share secrets with friends?** Yes, I do. Sometimes my friends and I tell each other our secrets. / No, I don't. I keep all my secrets to myself.

Q&A - 5 DO YOU EVER? - STUDENT B

- **Do you ever buy things and regret it later? (buyer's remorse)** No, I don't. I always research a product before buying it. / Yes, sometimes I buy something on impulse, only to regret it later.
- **Do you ever give money to charity or church?** No, I keep all my money for myself and spend it on my family. / Yes, I donate money to charity for someone in a difficult situation.
- **Do you ever forget the name of someone you've just met?** No, I don't. I have a photographic memory and remember everyone's names. / Yes, sometimes I forget a person's name and then it's embarrassing to ask them again.
- **Do you ever worry about the future of the planet?** No, I believe that the world will improve and become a better place. / Yes, I do. I often worry about pollution and overpopulation which is harmful to the environment.
- **Do you ever snore while sleeping?** No, I sleep deeply without snoring. Yes, when I snore my parents wake me up to stop.
- **Do you ever forget something, then go back to get it?** No, I always remember to take everything I need when leaving home. / Yes, I left home without my mask and had to return to fetch it.
- **Do you ever stalk someone online?** No, I never stalk people online. I only follow my friends on social media. / Yes. When I have a crush, I often check her Facebook and Instagram pages.
- **Do you ever copy homework from a friend?** No, I do my own, original work. / Yes. When I haven't done my homework, I borrow my friend's book and copy his answers.
- **Do you ever sing in the shower?** No, I have a terrible singing voice so I don't sing anywhere, not even in the shower. / Yes, the acoustics in the bathroom sound great, so I often sing in the shower.
- **Do you ever swear in public?** No, I never swear in public. / Yes, if something bad happens I might swear in public.

6 Holidays

QUESTIONS & ANSWERS STUDENT A

1. **Do you like holidays?** Yes, I like holidays because I get to spend time with my family. / No, I don't like holidays because I have to spend time with my family.

2. **Can you name two religious' holidays that you celebrate?** In my country we celebrate Easter and Christmas. These are Christian holidays.

3. **What public holidays do you have in your country?** Most countries have unique holidays where they have the day off and spend it at home. For example, many countries celebrate Worker's Day (Labor Day) on May 1st.

4. **Is it better to stay at home on holidays or go somewhere else?** I like to spend my holiday at home with my family. / I like to travel somewhere special on holidays because that is the only time I have off.

5. **What are some holidays celebrated all across the world?** There are many days that are becoming more common to celebrate all across the world. For example: Mother's Day, Father's Day and New Year's Day.

6. **Is there any music related to holidays that you know?** The most common example of holiday music is Christmas music. Especially Mariah Carey's "All I want for Christmas" is played nonstop in stores during December.

7. **What's your favorite holiday memory?** On Mother's Day, my brothers and I baked a cake for my mom. That is my favorite memory of a special day.

8. **Do you have any special family traditions around a holiday?** When I was young, the children in my family would put on a nativity play for the adults on Christmas.

9. **What was the best fireworks display that you've ever seen?** When the clock strikes 12 on New Year's Eve, many fireworks go off.

10. **What's the best gift you've received for a holiday?** When I was young, my dad got me a small radio as gift for summer vacation.

Q&A - 6 HOLIDAYS - STUDENT B

1. **What's your favorite holiday?** My favorite holiday is Christmas because I get to spend time with my family and receive presents.
2. **Where do you like to go for vacation?** I love going to the beach for vacation. I enjoy swimming in the ocean and playing on the sand. At the beach we eat lots of ice cream and enjoy playing volleyball or other games.
3. **What holiday food do you like?** During the Easter holiday, I like to eat hot-cross buns. It's a bun with a cross on top and raisins inside. It's great to eat with butter.
4. **Do you think holidays are too commercialized?** Some holidays like Christmas are too commercialized; meaning that companies are only using the holiday to market their products.
5. **What's on TV during holidays?** There are many kinds holiday movies. For example, during Christmas we traditionally watch movies with a Christmas theme, or during Valentine's Day we see romantic movies.
6. **Is there a religious holiday that is special to you?** I especially enjoy Christmas, but also like Easter because it allows me to reflect and think about my life and religion.
7. **Do you think holidays are important?** Yes, I especially enjoy Christmas, but also like Easter because it allows me to reflect and think about my life and religion.
8. **On which holiday do people decorate their houses?** Some popular holidays to decorate houses are Christmas, Thanksgiving and even though it's not a holiday, Halloween. People like putting up decorations to celebrate those special days.
9. **Is there a holiday connected to a person?** The majority of religious holidays in western culture are connected to Jesus, but there are some other special days that are connected to a person, for example Saint Patrick's Day.
10. **Do you ever visit relatives for a holiday?** Relatives are extended family. If possible, I like to have my whole family together to spend

time together.

7 Weather

QUESTIONS & ANSWERS STUDENT A

1. **What is your favorite season and why?** I love summer because I enjoy swimming at the beach. / I like winter because I enjoy staying warm and cozy at home. / During fall I enjoy hiking. / I like spring because it isn't too hot or too cold, just the right temperature.
2. **Does winter get very cold in your country? What do you wear?** When it gets very cold during winter I wear a thick coat, a beanie on my head, a scarf and warm gloves. / It doesn't get too cold. I only need to wear a sweater during winter.
3. **What area in your country has the best weather?** I live in South Korea and the southern part of the country is closer to the equator, which means that the weather is slightly warmer.
4. **Does your country have weather disasters such as tornadoes or typhoons?** Our country periodically gets hit with typhoons during the rainy season. When that happens, we stay indoors to keep safe.
5. **Can you describe the weather in your country?** We have four distinct seasons. It's hot in summer, cold in winter, cherry blossoms bloom during spring and people enjoy hiking when the leaves come down in fall.
6. **Why is it important to know the weather forecast?** It is important to know what weather to expect in order to know what clothes to wear and to plan for future events.
7. **Do you think the weather is changing?** Have you heard of global warming? Many scientists believe that the earth is getting warmer which is dangerous for our planet.
8. **How does weather impact your emotions?** When it rains on a cool day, I feel like staying home. Warm weather excites me so I want to be outside more.
9. **When it rains a lot, we say it is raining cats and dogs. Do you have an expression like that?** In Norway, they say "It's falling female trolls." In Greece, they say "It's raining chair legs."

10. **If you could control the weather, what would you do?** I would give farmers rain when they needed it so that they can harvest more food for the people.

Q&A - 7 WEATHER - STUDENT B

1. **What type of weather do you like the most?** I love sunny and warm weather because I can play outside without wearing too much clothing.
2. **What do you do on rainy days?** On rainy days I stay inside and play card games with my family.
3. **What is your favorite summer memory?** When I was young, we would go to my grandmother's house near the beach. We would stay at her home and swim at the beach daily. That is my favorite summer memory.
4. **The sun can be dangerous. How can we protect ourselves from harsh sunlight?** We can apply sunscreen on our skin and wear sunglasses for UV protection.
5. **What does it mean to be "under the weather"?** If you don't know, guess. It means that I don't feel very well. I feel sick or sad so I am not feeling my best.
6. **Have you ever worn the wrong clothes for the weather? Or have you forgotten an umbrella at home and it started to rain?** I went outside without my jacket and it became cold. I have gone outside without an umbrella and it started to rain.
7. **Has the weather ever made you cancel your plans?** A friend and I planned to go on a trip, but the day before we checked the weather to see that rain was expected. Following the weather report, we postponed our travel plan.
8. **What is the hottest temperature you've ever experienced?** The hottest temperature I have experienced was around 40 degrees Celsius during a heat wave. Because of the heat we stayed home and switched on the air-conditioning full blast!
9. **During which month does your country get the most rain?** Take a guess. My country gets the most rain during September.
10. **Have you ever seen snow? What activities can people do in snow?** Yes, I have seen snow. If it snows enough you can ski, build a snowman or have a snowball fight with friends.

8 Shopping

QUESTIONS & ANSWERS STUDENT A

- **What is the last thing you've bought?** The last thing I bought is the shirt I am wearing right now.
- **What is your favorite brand?** My favorite clothing brand is Adidas.
- **How do you feel about online shopping?** If you had $1000, what would you buy? I prefer online shopping because it is convenient and sometimes cheaper than the store price. / I don't like shopping online for clothes because sometimes the sizes don't match.
- **Have you ever bought something only to regret it later?** Yes, I bought some shoes that I hardly ever wear. I regret buying them.
- **Who does the shopping at your home? How often do they go shopping?** My mom usually does the grocery shopping. She goes shopping once a week.
- **If you had $1000, what would you buy?** I would buy a brand-new phone. / I would use the money to have a big party with my friends!
- **In general, why do women enjoy shopping more than men?** It could be because women enjoy showing off or looking for new things to buy.
- **A bargain hunter is someone who loves to find sales or discounts. Are you a bargain hunter?** Yes, I love searching for the best item at the lowest price. / No, I don't care about a bargain. If I really want something, I just buy it.
- **Shoplifting is when someone steals from a shop. How do shops prevent this from happening?** In most stores there is some kind of security like video cameras and on clothing there is a magnetic seal that you have to remove before leaving the store.
- **Where is a good place to go shopping in your city?** In the center of my city there is an area with lots of shops to buy from. That is the best place to go shopping.

Q&A - 8 SHOPPING - STUDENT B

1. **What is your favorite shop?** My favorite shop is a clothing store called Uniqlo. I like it because the style of the clothes is simple but made from quality material.
2. **What do you buy at least once a week?** At least once a week I go to a café and order a café latte.
3. **If you opened your own shop, what would you sell?** I would sell electronics such as computers and other gadgets.
4. **What groceries do you buy at the supermarket?** I buy meat, rice, vegetables, milk and eggs. I use the groceries to cook food.
5. **What is the most expensive thing you have ever bought?** My car is the most expensive thing I have bought, followed by my laptop.
6. **Do you prefer shopping alone or with friends?** I prefer shopping alone so I can take my time and walk around without being rushed. / I prefer shopping with friends so I can ask their opinion before buying something.
7. **Your birthday is tomorrow. What gift would you like to receive?** I would like to receive something practical like a new belt or cologne.
8. **What is something that is better to buy online?** Books are easy to buy online because they don't have different sizes, so it's the same as when you buy them in a store.
9. **In the United States, Black Friday is a day with many sales. Is there a special day in your country to go shopping?** In China they have Single's Day on November 11th, on that day they have many sales and online promotions. In other countries, Christmas is a popular time for sales because many people buy gifts.
10. **Have you ever returned an item to a shop? What and why?** Once I was given a shirt as a present, but it was the wrong size. So I returned and exchanged it for a shirt that is the correct size.

9 Movies

QUESTIONS & ANSWERS STUDENT A

1. **What's your favorite movie?** My favorite movie is *'Avengers'* because I like action scenes and superheroes. / My favorite movie is *'Forrest Gump'* because the main character is likeable and it has a really good story.
2. **How often do you go to the cinema?** I go to the cinema at least once a month. Whenever a big, blockbuster movie is released I go to watch it.
3. **Who are some of your favorite actors?** I really like Chris Hemsworth, the actor that plays Thor in Avengers. He is funny and works hard to get his body into amazing shape.
4. **When is the last time you've cried while watching a film?** Last year I watched a documentary called *'Dear Zachary'*. Something sad happened that made me cry.
5. **What is the most annoying thing someone can do in the cinema?** I hate hearing people talk in a cinema. Another pet peeve is when someone uses a phone during the movie.
6. **What movie sequel would you love to see? If you could watch a follow-up (or sequel) to a movie, what would it be?** It would be interesting to see the sequel to *'Forrest Gump'*. Unfortunately, production of the movie was canceled after the 9/11 attack.
7. **Who is the best movie hero (or protagonist)?** One of the biggest movie heroes is Ironman because he is the leader of the *'Avengers'*. At the end he sacrifices himself for the world.
8. **What is the worst movie you've ever seen?** There is a great cartoon series called 'Avatar: The Last Airbender'. They made a movie out of it that is really bad.
9. **Who do you like to watch movies with or do you like watching alone?** I prefer movies alone. / I like watching movies with my friends so we can share the excitement and make jokes during the film.
10. **Do you think age restrictions on movies are a good idea?** Is it bad for young people to watch violent movies? I think age-restricting movies is a good idea because it protects younger viewers from bad language,

excessive violence or nudity.

Q&A - 9 MOVIES - STUDENT B

1. **What movie genre do you like?** My favorite movie genre is action because I like to watch the characters fight for a greater goal.
2. **What is the best snack to eat while watching a movie?** The best snack to eat while watching a movie is popcorn as it is easy to eat. You just move the popcorn from the bag to your mouth without having to look.
3. **How many movies do you watch per week?** I watch a movie a week. I mostly watch on Netflix and occasionally at the cinema.
4. **What is the scariest movie you've ever watched?** I hate scary movies. One of the scariest movies I watched was 'Paranormal Activity'. You never see the monster, but psychologically it creates fear.
5. **What is more important in a movie, acting or special effects?** I believe that the story is the most important part of a movie. Good acting paired with a good story is much better than a movie that relies too much on special effects.
6. **If someone made a movie of your life, what kind of movie would it be?** If a movie was made about my life, it would be a rags-to-riches film, similar to the Will Smith' movie called 'The Pursuit of happiness'.
7. **Who is the best bad guy (or antagonist)?** The best villain is from *'Die Hard'*, Hans Gruber. The actor that played him is Alan Rickman, who sadly died in 2016.
8. **What character would you like to play in a movie?** Some people want to be a hero, some people want to be the villain. I would like to be an extra that dies in a funny way during a movie.
9. **What's better: Books or Movies?** Most people prefer books over movies as you get to know more about the story and you build it using your imagination. That being said, movies will always make more money than their book counterparts.
10. **Can you describe your favorite scene from a movie?** My favorite scene from a movie is in *'Avengers'*, where everyone is fighting in Wakanda against Thanos' army. The good guys are about to lose when Thor appears to save the day with Rocket and Groot.

10 Television

QUESTIONS & ANSWERS STUDENT A

1. **What TV show are you watching right now?** Currently I'm watching 'Grey's Anatomy'. It is a drama about doctors at a hospital.
2. **How much time do you spend watching TV every week?** Every week I watch about ten hours of television.
3. **What TV show genres do you know?** Dramas, Talk shows etc. There are many kinds of genres for TV shows: Drama, news, sport, comedy, action and thrillers.
4. **Who is a popular TV show character?** Sheldon from 'The Big Bang Theory' is a popular TV show character because he is very unique and funny.
5. **If you had your own TV show, what would it be about?** If I could create my own show, it would be some kind of Sci-fi Fantasy where characters travel between worlds and battle different enemies.
6. **What are some negatives about watching TV?** When people stay inside watching TV, they don't go outside for fresh air or get the exercise their bodies need.
7. **What would life be like without TV?** These days many people use their phones or computers as a replacement for TVs, so if TVs were to disappear it wouldn't have such a big effect on our lives.
8. **TV is a source of information. How can we use it positively?** The big problem with information from the news is that it is delivered with a bias. News networks present information in a way that they see fit, and it might not necessarily be correct.
9. **Every year there is a new trend on TV. What is a recent trend?** In South Korea there are reality TV shows showing a celebrity's 'real life', then a panel of experts comment on the footage.
10. **Do you ever watch shows in another language? What shows?** I enjoy watching Japanese animation such as 'Naruto' with English subtitles.

Q&A - 10 TELEVISION - STUDENT B

- **Do you use Netflix? What is your favorite show?** Occasionally I watch Netflix for one of my favorite shows, 'The Umbrella Academy'. The first season was great but the second a bit of a let-down.
- **What TV show would you suggest for a friend to watch?** For young people I would suggest 'Avatar: The last Airbender" and for adults I would recommend 'MasterChef: The Professionals', a cooking show.
- **How do you watch TV: On a television, computer, tablet or phone**? I watch most of my content on my computer. It's easy to switch between work and read articles while watching Netflix or YouTube.
- **What is your opinion on television? Is it good or bad?** Television is great for sharing information and entertaining people of all ages. The negative is that people waste too much of their lives in front of the TV instead of being productive and going outside.
- **If you could be any character in a TV show, who would it be?** I would like to be the host of a TV game show and be the one asking questions to contestants while making funny remarks in between.
- **Is too much TV bad for young people?** Yes, young people need to play and use their imaginations instead of watching too much TV. They should read more books and play outside with friends to exercise and practice social skills.
- **How will TV change in the next couple of decades?** I believe that TV will become more interactive which means that the viewer will have more control over what happens in a program.
- **What is your opinion on reality TV?** Reality TV shows people in 'real life'. It is very easy to make because you don't need actors or a story, but a lot of it is faked to make it more interesting.
- **What time of the day do most people watch TV?** Most people watch TV in the evenings to relax after a day's work.
- **If you could create your own TV network, what shows would you have on?** If I had my own TV channel it would have all my favorite programs: Mostly action and comedy shows. It will also include some livestreams to keep the audience up-to-date.

11 Fashion

QUESTIONS & ANSWERS STUDENT A

1. **What clothes are you wearing today?** Today I am wearing a white shirt with blue jeans.
2. **How many pairs of shoes do you own?** I own five pairs of shoes.
3. **Are you interested in fashion?** I appreciate good fashion but I prefer wearing comfortable clothes.
4. **What is your favorite piece of clothing?** My favorite piece of clothing is my leather jacket. I wear it during spring and fall.
5. **What kind of fashion interests you most – clothes, hair, cosmetics, shoes, accessories?** I don't use cosmetics and I'm not fussy about my hair. Besides wearing a watch, I don't really care for accessories so the only area of fashion I am interested in is clothing.
6. **Do you think you have too many or not enough clothes at home?** I have too many clothes at home, but I always wear the same clothes over-and-over again.
7. **Think about yourself when you were younger, were you stylish?** No! When I was young, I followed many temporary trends which are really bad when I think about it now.
8. **What are some past fashion trends in your country?** In the past, many teenage boys had a center parting in their hair - a trend that was caused by Leonardo Di Caprio in the movie, Titanic.
9. **Do you thinking learning to put on make-up is a valuable skill?** In today's modern world, appearance is more important than ever because we take many photos and videos that appear on social media. Therefore, we are more aware about how look, causing people to use make-up more skillfully. Being good at applying make-up is a valuable skill.
10. **Can you tell me about a big event that you had to dress up for?** A few months ago, I attended a friend's wedding where I had to wear a suit. Formal wear is required at certain events.

Q&A - 11 FASHION - STUDENT B

1. **What did you wear yesterday?** Yesterday I wore a grey sweater and dark pants.
2. **What is your most expensive piece of clothing?** Last year I bought a new suit which is my most expensive piece of clothing.
3. **Can you describe your fashion style?** My fashion style is very simple with basic colors. I usually wear jeans with V-neck t-shirts in black, white or blue.
4. **Do you have a favorite fashion brand? Why do you like it?** I like to wear Adidas sneakers because I also enjoy their simple design.
5. **If you could change anything about your style, what would it be?** I wish I looked more professional when wearing semi-casual clothes in public.
6. **Does fashion need to be expensive to be good?** No, fashion doesn't need to be expensive to look good. You can get affordable clothing that suits your style and fits well for your figure.
7. **Retro means an old fashion that has become popular again. Can you think of any examples?** These days I see many young people wearing colorful sweaters. That is a popular trend from the 80's that is becoming popular again.
8. **What are some recent fashion trends that you've spotted?** This past winter, I've seen many people wear fleece jackets with a large square on the left breast. This is very popular here in South Korea at the moment.
9. **Do you have someone whose fashion style you admire?** There are many celebrities that are very stylish when they appear in public. I wish I looked as good as they do so I will try to copy their style.
10. **Do your parents dislike some clothing that you wear? What and why?** When I was young my parents disliked my fashion choices and clothes that I wore, but these days they don't mind what I wear.

12 Emotions

QUESTIONS & ANSWERS STUDENT A

- **How do you feel right now?** Right now, I feel happy / bored / focused.
- **What do you like to do when you get bored?** I like to lay on my bed and play with my phone.
- **Do you think animals have feelings?** Yes, I think animals have feelings. Especially intelligent animals such as cats, dogs and dolphins. But I don't think animals like fish have feelings.
- **Can you talk about a time when you were embarrassed?** Once, while on my way to school, I spilt coffee all over my shirt. I had to teach class with a big coffee stain on my chest.
- **Are you excited about anything coming up in the future?** I am excited at the idea of the world opening up so we can travel again.
- **Can money buy happiness?** No, money can't buy happiness. The most important things in life are free. / Yes, money can buy happiness. All my problems can be solved with a lot of money.
- **What makes you angry?** I can angry when someone cheats me. Another pet peeve is when someone walks slowly in front of me.
- **Do you enjoy spending time alone? What do you do?** I don't mind being by myself. When I am alone, I do extra work or read a book.
- **Are women more emotional than men?** I'm not sure if that is true, but as men it is expected of us not to show our emotions.
- **Some people say 'Love is the greatest emotion'. Do you think it's true?** I think love is the most powerful emotion because it makes us do great things. It is a positive force in the universe.

Q&A - 12 EMOTIONS - STUDENT B

1. **What makes you nervous or anxious?** If I have a big test ahead and I haven't prepared enough, I get anxious.
2. **Do you like to watch scary movies?** Why or why not? I love watching

scary movies because I like the feeling you get when you see something scary. / I hate watching scary movies because it bothers me and stops me from sleeping well at night.

3. **What do you do to relax?** I like to take short walks in nature to relax.
4. **Is it better to hide or show your anger?** I guess it depends. Usually, anger stops you from making clear decisions. But other times anger can show people your true emotions.
5. **Tell me about a time you felt really happy?** On Christmas I received a thoughtful gift from a friend. It made me very happy.
6. **What is a memory that makes you smile?** I have a beautiful memory of my family sharing a meal. Every time I think of that, it makes me smile.
7. **If you have a problem, who do you talk to?** If I have a big problem and I need to talk to someone to, I call my best friend and they give me advice.
8. **Have you ever been in love? How did it feel?** Yes, I've been in love before. It is the best and worst feeling you can get. When the love is returned it is the best and it is the worst when it is one-sided love.
9. **What emotion do you wish you could control better?** I wish I could control my regret better. I think about situations in the past which brings up a lot of regret. Life would be easier if I could let go of what happened in the past.
10. **EQ is emotional intelligence. Who is someone in your life that has high EQ?** My friend really understands how to work with other people. She quickly understands how they feel and how to respond to their feelings. I wish I had her emotional intelligence.

13 Health

QUESTIONS & ANSWERS STUDENT A

1. **How often do you catch a cold?** I usually catch a cold during the winter. / I am very healthy; I don't get sick often.
2. **How do you exercise to keep fit?** After waking up, I stretch and do yoga. / I go for a daily walk outside. / I exercise at the gym three times a week.
3. **Have you ever had stiches?** I had an accident where I cut my hand and received three stitches.
4. **What are some of the dangerous diseases in the world?** Unfortunately, many people suffer from cancer, diabetes, HIV and COVID.
5. **How can you prevent getting sick?** You should keep healthy by eating good food or taking supplements. Also, stay away from sick people and be hygienic by washing your hands often.
6. **Are people healthier now than 100 years ago?** People are definitely healthier than 100 years ago thanks to improvements in medicine. The average person's life-expectancy has risen by 20 to 30 years.
7. **How can you improve your health?** You can improve your health by following a healthy diet. You should eat more fruits, vegetables, lean meats, grains, and less sugary and baked items. Also exercise to keep in shape.
8. **What can you do if you have trouble sleeping?** If you have trouble sleeping you should turn off lights, keep away from computers and phones an hour before bed, don't drink anything with sugar or caffeine like coffee a few hours before you plan on sleeping.
9. **Living long is also because of genetics. How old do people in your family become?** On my father's side of my family, most people live to around 70 and 80 years of age. On my mother's side they live a bit longer.
10. **What are some jobs that are hazardous (bad) for a person's health?** Being in an unhealthy environment like working dangerous chemicals.

Also, many jobs require us to sit down and be in a stationary position. Sitting down for too long isn't good for our physical wellbeing.

Q&A - 13 HEALTH - STUDENT B

- **When is the last time you went to the doctor?** I went to the doctor two weeks ago because I had an eye infection. He gave me antibiotics to take for a couple of days.
- **What foods are good for your health?** You should eat lots of fruits, vegetables, whole grains and lean proteins. Try and stay away from baked products and sugary foods.
- **Have you ever broken a bone?** No, I have never broken a bone. / Yes, I have broken my arm before. I had to go to the hospital to get a cast.
- **What illnesses have you had?** I've had the flu, the cold and chicken pox. I've been fortunate not to catch any dangerous diseases.
- **Why is smoking bad for you?** Smoking is bad for your lungs and your cardiovascular system, but it affects many parts of your body. It is advisable to quit smoking or even better, never to start smoking if you haven't yet. When you smoke, you become addicted and constantly obsess about it.
- **Do you think happy people live longer? Why?** When you are happy, your brain releases lots of chemicals that are good for body. Happier people have stronger hearts and are more resistant to diseases.
- **How often do you go to the dentist?** I go to the dentist twice a year for a check-up.
- **Why is too much stress unhealthy?** Too much stress is bad for our hearts. It raises our blood pressure and gives a lot of anxiety, which means that a person is more likely to suffer a heart attack.
- **These days people are worried about catching COVID. How can we stay safe?** You should social-distance from other people. Also take care of your hygiene by wearing a mask and frequently washing your hands.
- **What medicine or first aid do you have at home?** In my home I have Tylenol for headaches and band-aids in case I cut myself. Other medicines include eyedrops and ointments to apply in case of infection.

14 Music

QUESTIONS & ANSWERS STUDENT A

1. **What is your favorite type of music?** My personal type of music is pop and rock, but there are many good songs from other genres that I also enjoy listening to.
2. **Where do you usually listen to music?** I enjoy listening to music on my car radio. These days many people listen to music on streaming services such as Spotify. If I am with friends, we watch music videos on YouTube.
3. **Have you ever been to a concert?** I really enjoy going to live concerts. In the past I have been to K-pop and rock concerts.
4. **Can you play a musical instrument?** I think it is a great skill to learn a musical instrument such as piano, violin or guitar. Unfortunately, I can't play any musical instruments.
5. **What music do your parents listen to?** My parents' taste in music is much different from my own. They prefer gospel and traditional music.
6. **If you could meet any musician (from the past or present), who would it be?** Musicians usually have interesting personalities. If I could meet any musician, it would be Frank Sinatra.
7. **Who is the most famous singer from your country?** The most famous musician in South Korea is Psy, but right now BTS is one of the most popular groups in the world.
8. **If you could stop any genre of music, which one would you ban?** If I could stop any genre, it would be techno or heavy metal because they are too noisy.
9. **Do you listen to any musical groups from other countries?** The majority of international music comes from the United States. I enjoy listening to is a rock group called Foo Fighters.
10. **What is more important, lyrics or sound?** Some music has beautiful lyrics, but I believe that sound and beat are more important to a song because some songs are popular even though I have no idea what they are singing.

Q&A - 14 MUSIC - STUDENT B

1. **Who is your favorite musician or singer?** These days I enjoy listening to Post Malone and Ed Sheeran.
2. **How often do you listen to music?** I don't listen to music very often, but when I do, I am outside or with friends.
3. **What live performance would you like to see?** I would like to see a big rock concert. Something like Metallica.
4. **Do you have a favorite band?** My favorite international band is called Foo Fighters.
5. **How has music changed from the previous generation?** Like everything in life, things are constantly changing. Music has changed a lot from the previous generation. We can find music online and on social media apps like TikTok. Music has also become more modern by using computer-generated sounds instead of musical instruments.
6. **What app do you use to listen to music?** Most people listen to music on the Spotify app. I also like to watch music videos on YouTube when I am with friends.
7. **Would you like to be a famous singer? Why/Why not?** Yes, I would like to be a great singer because it would make me rich and famous. I can share many ideas and emotions through my music.
8. **What is a song that is currently very popular?** These days 'Blinding Lights' from 'The Weekend' is a popular song that can often be heard on the radio.
9. **Are you a good singer? What is your go-to song?** No, I am a really bad singer. When I go to a karaoke room, I like to sing songs from 'My Way' by Frank Sinatra because it's an easier song for men to sing.
10. **Do you think your taste in music will change when you get older?** I don't think so. Music will change but my taste will remain the same.

15 Hobbies

QUESTIONS & ANSWERS STUDENT A

1. **What hobbies do you have?** I enjoy reading books and exercising. / My hobbies include playing computer games, watching Netflix and playing football with my friends.
2. **If you had more free time, how would you spend it?** If I had more free time, I would like to meet my friends and hang out. / If I had more free time, I would spend it by learning a new language.
3. **Do you think people should have hobbies?** Yes, hobbies are important to keep ourselves happy. Every person is unique with their own tastes and interests. We pursue our interests through our hobbies.
4. **What is an activity that you would like to do in the future?** I would like to try a new activity such as boxing or surfing. It would also be nice to play a musical instrument or learn a new language.
5. **How do you spend your evenings?** I spend my evenings at home making dinner, watching TV, browsing the internet or checking social media on my phone.
6. **What are some expensive hobbies that you know of?** Some expensive hobbies include yachting, skiing or other activities that require expensive equipment.
7. **Can a hobby be dangerous?** Yes, some hobbies are more dangerous than others. For example, skydiving is more dangerous than badminton.
8. **Does your hobby influence what friends you have?** Yes, it is natural to make friends around a similar hobby. Because you have the same interest you can talk about it and share your passions and experiences related to that hobby.
9. **What hobbies do many women in your country have? Shopping?** Just kidding. Women have very interesting and exciting hobbies such as photography, fitness and travel, just like men.
10. **Do you ever feel like you are wasting your free time? How?** When I was young, I wasted a lot of my free time playing computer games. Instead of doing something productive, I spent hours playing games which

never had a positive impact on my life. There should be a balance between doing things which improve your life, and other hobbies meant for relaxation and fun.

Q&A - 15 HOBBIES - STUDENT B

1. **What do you do in your free time?** In my free time I like to meet up with my friends and when I am alone, I enjoy watching YouTube videos.
2. **What is a cheap hobby that anyone can do?** Most hobbies are quite cheap when starting out. You can draw, do graphic design or coding on a computer, use your phone for taking photos or learn a new language.
3. **How many hours do you spend on your hobby every week?** I spend about an hour or two on my hobby every day and on weekends it is more.
4. **What hobbies did you have when you were young?** When I was young, I enjoyed stamp collecting. My friends and family would bring me stamps from all over the world when they visited me.
5. **What are some interesting hobbies that you know of?** I think that some interesting hobbies involve DIY (Do It Yourself) projects. A hobby where you create something like woodwork or knitting. Those are interesting because they rely on creativity and the production of something new.
6. **What hobbies are popular in your country?** These days a lot of women are interest in improving their make-up skills. Other people try blogging or photography. Another recent trend that many young people follow is getting into their best physical shape to take profile photos.
7. **What do you do on weekends?** On weekends I enjoy hiking or traveling to interesting places. I also drive to different places to go sightseeing.
8. **Can you make money doing a hobby?** Yes, when you do a hobby, you are improving your skills. Other people can pay you for teaching or doing it as a service. Especially if you create something or become a master at a marketable skill.
9. **What are some popular hobbies for men in your country?** Men enjoy outdoor activities such as football, fishing and rock climbing.
10. **What is a good hobby for a boyfriend or girlfriend to have?** In my

humble opinion, I would appreciate a girlfriend that is good at cooking since I am not that good. A boyfriend should enjoy photography so he can take beautiful photos of his girlfriend, or cooking also helps.

16 Crime

QUESTIONS & ANSWERS - STUDENT A

- **What phone number do you dial to reach the police in your country?** If you have an emergency in South Korea, you can reach the emergency services by dialing 119. It is the reverse of the United States where the emergency number is 911.
- **Has anyone ever stolen something from you?** When I was young, someone tried to pickpocket my wallet, but I was able to get it back.
- **Why do people go to prison?** People go to prison when they do something illegal. It could be anything from selling drugs to murder, then they spend more time in prison according to the severity of the crime.
- **Do you think criminals can change?** Yes, people can change, and criminals are people too. Therefore, if they have remorse and show a willingness to change, it is possible.
- **What is a common crime in your country?** A recent common crime is tax-evasion. Tax-evasion is when someone tries to cheat the government out of taxes.
- **Are you afraid of being the victim of a crime?** Yes, I am afraid of being a victim of a crime. One should always be careful and vigilant, especially in unknown areas.
- **What do you know about internet crime?** Personal information on the internet is increasing. If someone gets hold of your personal banking information, they could steal your money. As more people move online, internet crimes will increase.
- **Should police be more, or less strict?** Police reaction depends on the situation. In light cases they should not deal to harshly, but when people's lives are at stake, they should react more severely.
- **What kind of crimes do you worry about when you travel abroad?** When I travel abroad, I worry about someone cheating me or stealing my wallet. We should take care of our belongings while traveling.
- **Do you think that 'crime pays'?** No. Crime never pays, petty crimes only help a criminal temporarily. There is also the risk of getting caught

and then being sent to jail.

Q&A - 16 CRIME - STUDENT B

1. **Is your country safe?** Currently I live in South Korea, one of the safest countries in the world. You could leave your laptop in a café for an hour, upon returning it would still be there. My country of origin is South Africa, there you have to be more careful about your belongings.
2. **What is an important law that everyone should follow?** Laws for the road are very important. By disobeying road laws many people's lives are put at risk - Those of drivers and pedestrians that walk in the street.
3. **What are some crimes that you know?** There are many types of crimes like murder, stealing, kidnapping, violence, tax-evasion and destruction of property.
4. **Do you know what shoplifting is? What kind of items do criminals steal?** Shoplifting is stealing small items from a shop. Most items are snacks or clothes, anything small enough to be hidden and carried outside.
5. **If you could steal anything without being caught, what would it be?** If I could steal anything without being caught, I would steal an expensive car.
6. **Did you ever want to be a police officer? Why / Why not?** No, I've never wanted to be a police officer because it is a difficult, dangerous job and I don't think it would suit my personality.
7. **Juvenile crime is when young people commit crime. What kind of crimes do young people typically commit?** Young people commit crimes such as assault, stealing, vandalism (destroying property) or using illegal drugs.
8. **Do movies and TV programs show what real criminals look like?** In movies and TV shows, characters are black or white, good or bad. But the real world is more like gray, where some people are not 100% good nor 100% evil. So no, I don't believe that the media reflects how criminals really are.
9. **What causes a person to commit a crime?** Most criminals are made by their environment. If they grow up in a difficult neighborhood and have no positive role models, they are more likely to turn to a life of crime.

10. **Do you have any crime prevention tips?** Stay safe by being aware of your environment. Be vigilant, especially in more dangerous areas. Lock your doors and take care of your possessions.

17 Dating

QUESTIONS & ANSWERS STUDENT A

- **Why do people go on dates?** People go on dates to get to know each other. If they like the other person, they can start a relationship. People date to find a partner.
- **How would you ask someone on a date?** There are many ways to ask someone on a date, but first, try to get to know the person before asking for a date.
- **What is your idea of an ideal date?** My idea of a perfect date is going for a nice dinner then a walk afterwards, especially in an interesting place with many things talk about.
- **Do you believe in love at first sight? Why or why not?** Love at first sight is when you immediately fall in love when you see someone. We are attracted to appearance, but fall in love with personality. So, I don't believe in love and first sight.
- **Who is your celebrity crush?** My celebrity crush is Blake Lively. She is tall and beautiful but unfortunately for me, already married to Ryan Reynolds.
- **What does it mean to 'go Dutch'?** Traditionally, when going on a date a man would pay. But these days, men and women are equal so when you 'go Dutch', you split the bill.
- **Have you ever been to a wedding? What happened?** Yes, I have been to a wedding before. Families join to share in the happiness of the couple getting married. Everyone dresses up for the occasion and there is a ceremony to seal the marriage.
- **How long should you date someone before getting married?** Each couple is different - It could be one to ten years.
- **What positives are there to being married?** Being married is a union between two partners that love and support each other. Together you can start a family and grow old together.
- **Why do you think so many people get divorced these days?** These days many couples get divorced. There are many reasons for it: falling out of

love, arguing and abuse are the main reasons.

Q&A - 17 DATING - STUDENT B

1. **Where do people usually go on dates?** People usually go to restaurants, parks or malls for a date. Those places have interesting activities that a couple can do together.
2. **Describe your ideal partner?** My ideal partner is beautiful, family-orientated and mutually supportive of each other's goals.
3. **What is your idea of a bad date?** A bad date is one where the other person doesn't put in any effort to get to know you, like spending all the time on their phone.
4. **Do you have a boyfriend or girlfriend?** No, I don't have a girlfriend at the moment. I am single. / Yes, I have a girlfriend. Her name is Jenna.
5. **What is a blind date?** A blind date is where a date was organized for you by someone else, and you haven't met your date yet. Co-workers, friends or family might set you up on a blind date with someone.
6. **Do you want to get married?** Yes, I would like to get married to the right person. / No, I'm not interested in marriage. I'm enjoying my life as it is.
7. **Do you know any wedding traditions from your country?** In South Africa we have mostly western styled weddings. After the wedding ceremony is a reception where everyone celebrates by drinking and dancing. At the end of the party, the bride throws the bouquet of flowers behind her to girls wishing to get married.
8. **What negatives are there to being married?** When you are married, you are committed that person. So, you have to make sure that it is the right person for you.
9. **An arranged marriage is when your parents choose your partner. Would you want your parents to arrange a marriage for you?** I don't think so. My parents know me very well and know my personality. But we may have different tastes in people.
10. **How can you make yourself more attractive to members of the opposite sex?** To be a more attractive person you can work on your appearance, improve your personal communication people and increase

your valuable in life by learning new skills and acquiring assets like money.

18 Favorites

QUESTIONS & ANSWERS - STUDENT A

1. **What's your favorite color?** My favorite color is blue so most of my clothes are also dark blue. I believe it's a relaxing color that reflects a peaceful atmosphere.
2. **What's your favorite movie?** My favorite movie is *Forest Gump*. It has an interesting storyline and great acting by Tom Hanks.
3. **Who is your favorite singer or band?** I like pop and alternative music. These days I listen to Ed Sheeran. His music is touching and easy to dance to.
4. **What's your favorite restaurant?** These days my favorite restaurant is a Japanese restaurant not too far from where I live. The dish I order most of the time is called cheese tonkatsu, or pork cutlet.
5. **What's your favorite app on your phone?** My favorite app on my phone is 9gag. It allows users to share funny memes, videos and pictures.
6. **Who is your favorite athlete?** My favorite athlete is a UFC fighter called Israel Adesanya. He is a great striker that has an exciting fighting style.
7. **What's your favorite ice cream flavor?** When I go to Baskin Robbins, I usually order an ice cream flavor called 'My mom is an alien', an ice cream with chocolate, vanilla and chocolate- coated honeycomb balls on the inside.
8. **Who is your favorite TV or movie character?** My favorite character is from a Japanese animation, One Piece, called Zorro. He is a popular swordsman in the story that uses three swords at the same time and has green hair. The reason I like him is because he has a cool personality and trains hard to become the strongest swordsman in the world.
9. **What's your favorite way to relax?** I love going to the beach. After swimming for a long time, I return to the parasol and relax on a towel.
10. **What's your favorite memory of school?** When I was in elementary school, we would have a spring walk around the school. Parents would sponsor you for how many times you could circle the school It was a fun day without studies and an enjoyable way to celebrate the beginning of

spring.

Q&A - 18 FAVORITES - STUDENT B

- **What's your favorite animal?** When I was young, we had many dogs, I used to love playing and training them. I don't have a dog right now, but I would love to get one in the future.
- **Who is your favorite celebrity?** My favorite celebrity is a singer called Post Malone. He has tattoos all over his body that goes with his care-free attitude. I like his music and he has an interesting personality, but I wouldn't follow his style.
- **What's your favorite sport?** My favorite sport is rugby. It is a physical team sport with 15 players on a team. I played rugby when I was young, but now I only watch games on TV. I support the South African national rugby team and was especially happy when they won the Rugby World Cup in 2019.
- **What's your favorite fast food?** Hamburgers are one of my favorite foods. I go to McDonald's once or twice a month and order a burger set with Coke and fries.
- **What's your favorite TV show?** It might be surprising, but my favorite TV show is a reality show called MasterChef: The Professionals. In it professional chefs compete to be the best. Even though I can't cook very well, I enjoy seeing their passion and listening to them talk about the ingredients and processes involved.
- **What's your favorite brand?** My favorite clothing brand is Adidas. I always wear Adidas sneakers because they are simple and comfortable.
- **What's your favorite book?** The Lord of the Rings is my favorite book. It has wonderful characters and an interesting story filled with action and adventure.
- **Where is your favorite place to hang out with your friends?** Once every couple of weeks I meet my friends at a place called Gina's. We hang out, drink a beer and eat chicken. The owner knows us well and it has a nice atmosphere to have conversations.
- **Who is your favorite relative (family member)?** I enjoy spending time with my brother. We understand each other very well and we always have a great time no matter what we do.

9. **What's your favorite holiday experience?** I had an amazing time when I traveled to the Philippines. While I was there, I went to an island to surf and enjoy the peaceful lifestyle.

19 Travel

QUESTIONS & ANSWERS STUDENT A

- **Have you ever been abroad (to another country)?** Yes, I've been to other countries before. Last vacation I traveled to the Philippines. / No, I have never been abroad, but I would love to travel to Japan in the future.
- **Where did you go for you last vacation?** Last vacation I traveled to the Philippines. I had a great time! I ate good food, met interesting people and spent a lot of time surfing.
- **What do many people do during winter vacation?** During winter vacation many people go skiing or snowboarding while other people prefer staying in their warm homes.
- **What famous or historical place would you like to visit?** I would love to visit the Eiffel tower. It is such a historical monument that millions of people have visited. I would like to be one of them.
- **Where did you go on the last trip with your family? How was it?** The last trip I took with my mom and dad was to the beach. We went swimming, relaxed on the sand and had dinner at a nice restaurant in the evening.
- **Do you like relaxing vacations or exciting ones?** Sometimes we need relaxing vacations where you sit on the beach without doing a lot. Other times we need excitement and do fun activities. I think the ideal thing to do is have a mix of both relaxation and excitement so that you can regain some energy but also make memories.
- **What items should you take on vacation?** It depends where you are going: When going to a warm place you should take sunscreen and clothes that are suitable for the warm climate. If you go to a cold place, you should take a coat and gloves. Regardless of where you are going, you should remember your passport, wallet and chargers for your electronic devices.
- **What are some good travel tips?** Always make sure to plan your vacation ahead of time and organize travel insurance. Be mindful of your safety and belongings.

8. **What is something bad that happened to you while on vacation?** On my last vacation I got the flu while traveling. It was very uncomfortable and I was unsure where the hospitals were. I had to stay in my room for a week to recover. I'm happy I made it through that difficult experience.
9. **What souvenirs have you bought while traveling?** When I go traveling, I usually buy souvenirs for my friends and family. I always buy my mom a small doll that represents the country.

Q&A - 19 TRAVEL - STUDENT B

1. **What country would you like to visit in the future?** I would love to visit Hungary. I've heard that they have good food, interesting architecture and that the people are very friendly.
2. **What is the best place to visit in your country for summer?** I love going to the beach during summer. There I can swim to cool down and play fun sports on the sand.
3. **What is your preferred way to travel (plane, ship, car, bike)?** It depends where you are going. If you go somewhere nearby you should walk or go by bicycle. If it is more than an hour away, you should travel by car. If your destination is on an island, you can use a boat and if you are visiting another country, a plane would be your best option.
4. **What adventurous activity would you like to try in the future?** In the future I would like to learn kitesurfing. It looks difficult but extremely fun.
5. **Is it better to travel alone or with friends? Why?** Sometimes we have to travel alone to become more independent and experience things on our own. But it is more fun to travel with friends to make memories and enjoy the trip together.
6. **What is the most interesting food you've eaten on vacation?** I am normally picky about eating new foods but once, one a trip, we went diving for fish and seafood. As soon as we returned to shore, we cooked all the food we had caught.
7. **What do you have to plan before going on vacation?** You need to prepare your itinerary which includes your flights, accommodation, restaurants, documentation such as visas and activities you would like to do. Planning for success is important in life, and also when going on a

trip.
8. **Can you tell me about a fun travel story?** A number of years ago I went to Russia and I had an amazing time. The only problem was that I made a mistake and missed my flight home, which means that I had to redo my visa. In one day, I had to travel across the city and sort out this issue, then return to the airport to go home. It was a nerve-wrecking experience but I am happy that I made it through it.
9. **What do you like to do while traveling? Shop, relax, or sightsee?** I love sightseeing, doing fun activities and going to good restaurants. Therefore, I prefer places where there are a lot of new people to meet.
10. **What is your favorite photo that you have taken on vacation?** Tell me about it. When I was running through the city in Russia (Vladivostok), I stopped at a big statue in the middle of a public square to take a selfie. I was sweaty and tired but so grateful that I sorted out my visa to go back home. Every time I look at that photo, I feel a sense of relief.

20 Would you rather?

QUESTIONS & ANSWERS STUDENT A

- **Would you rather have a pet dinosaur or pet unicorn?** I would rather have a pet dinosaur because it is big and scary. / I would rather have a pet unicorn because it is beautiful and I can ride it.
- **Would you rather be rich or world famous?** I would rather be famous than rich because if I were famous, I could always earn more money.
- **Would you rather be blind or deaf (can't hear)?** I would rather be blind because I love listening to music. It would make me sad if I couldn't hear my mom's voice. / I would rather be deaf than blind because I would miss seeing all the beautiful things and scenery in the world.
- **Would you rather have three wishes in ten years, or one wish now?** I would rather wait and have three wishes in ten years. That way I will have more wishes to use and time to carefully think about what I should wish for next.
- **Would you rather have forever summer or forever winter?** I would rather have summer forever because I could go swimming and walk outside while wearing shorts. / I would choose winter because I can always wear more clothes and don't sweat as much.
- **Would you rather dance in front of 100 people or sing in front of 1,000 people?** I prefer singing in front of 1,000 people because I enjoy singing and I could pick and easy song that the audience might enjoy. Dancing is hard work.
- **Would you rather have an elephant-sized cat or a cat-sized elephant?** I would prefer a cat-sized elephant because it will be less dangerous than an elephant-sized cat! A mini elephant would also be very cute.
- **Would you rather speak every language in the world or have the ability to talk with animals?** I would rather want the ability to speak to animals. Languages can be translated, but no person can communicate with animals.
- **Would you rather go to the beach or the mountains during summer?** I would rather go to the beach during summer because I can tan on the

beach, play in the sand and swim in the ocean.

9. **Would you rather borrow $10,000 from your parents or $1,000 from your friends?** I would rather borrow $10,000 from my parents because they can trust that I will pay them back. Friends may want to have their money back sooner.

Q&A - 20 WOULD YOU RATHER? - STUDENT B

1. **Would you rather be invisible or able to fly?** There are many flying machines, but I would be the only invisible man. / I would like to fly because that would give me the ability to travel anywhere.
2. **Would you rather go without TV or fast food for the rest of your life?** I would rather go without wasting my time on watching TV. / I would rather stop eating fast food because TV is a source of entertainment and information.
3. **Would you rather see the future or change the past?** I prefer seeing into the future to take advantage of that knowledge. The past has happened to us but we can still change the future.
4. **Would you rather be a sport star (athletic) or a genius?** I would rather be a sport star because they make lots of money and are famous. / I prefer being a genius because I can make new discoveries that might improve the world.
5. **Would you rather be rich and ugly or good looking and poor?** I would rather be rich and ugly because beauty fades anyway, but well-managed wealth can last a long time.
6. **Would you rather be a famous inventor or a great writer?** I would rather be a famous inventor to improve the world. / Writers can create works that inspire people or make them dream.
7. **Would you rather only eat your favorite food for the rest of your life, or never be able to eat your favorite food again?** I would rather eat different foods than my favorite because there are thousands of different dishes to try, so I can find a new favorite food.
8. **Would you rather be a policeman or a firefighter?** I would rather be a police officer because there are a variety of jobs I could do. / I would rather be a firefighter because I want to save lives in emergencies.

9. **Would you rather live without your phone for two weeks or your computer for a month?** I would rather be without my phone for two weeks. I can access messaging apps and social media from my computer. Also, doing written assignments and projects is easier on a computer. / I would rather have my phone for a month. I need my phone when moving around so I am able to contact friends and have access to information.
10. **Would you rather have the world know about your finances or your love life?** I would rather have the world know about my money, because the government already knows about it. So, I would keep my love life private.

21 Time

QUESTIONS & ANSWERS STUDENT A

- **What time do you normally wake up?** I usually wake up at 8 am, but on weekends I wake up at around 9. I try to wake up early in the morning, but some days I sleep late.
- **What is your favorite time of the day?** My favourite time of the day is right before I fall asleep at night, because at that time I relax, check my phone for a last time and text goodnight to some friends.
- **How much free time do have?** When I was a student, I didn't have a lot of free time. Now, except for working, I have more free time to devote to my hobbies and do things I that enjoy.
- **Why does time fly when you are having fun?** When you are having fun, it feels as if time is going by more quickly. If you are bored, you are constantly waiting for time to pass, so it feels much longer.
- **Are you always on time?** Talk about the last time you were late. I prefer being at an appointment five minutes early. That way I'm always on time. I get very anxious when I'm not on time for an appointment. Before I arrive late, I send a message to let the person know.
- **What do you think will be the best time of your life and why? (When you were a child, a student or an adult?)** We should learn to enjoy every moment. Each time of our lives has some advantages and other disadvantages.
- **Every human has the same amount of time. How can you spend your time more efficiently?** I believe in making the most of our time. So, when you're busy, working towards something that will improve your life, that is time well spent.
- **What time is it now?** Right now, it is 3:50 pm. Or I can say it's ten to four in the afternoon.
- **How long does it take you to get ready for school?** It usually takes me about thirty minutes to get ready for school. I take a shower, get dressed, collect all the things that I need for class and then go to school.
- **One billion seconds = 32 years. Where do you see yourself in 32 years?**

In thirty-two years, I see myself in retirement with my wife, living an amazing life somewhere near the beach. Fingers crossed.

Q&A - 21 TIME - STUDENT B

- **What time do you usually go to bed?** I usually try to go to bed at around midnight, but I usually stay up a little later until 1 am.
- **What do you do during your free time?** During my free time I like to relax by watching something on YouTube or going for a walk. At least three a week I also go to the gym to get some exercise.
- **"Time = money" Do you agree?** Yes, I believe that every person has time to do what they want to do. But if you want to be successful you've got to apply yourself and use your time wisely.
- **What is your busiest day of the week? Why?** My busiest time of the week is usually on a Monday because that's when the work week starts. I have to make sure my classes are planned and that everything at home is ready for the week ahead.
- **If you could stop time, what would you do?** If I could stop time, I would use that time to learn a new skill or study new things. Also, if I could stop time, I could travel to different places without wasting time and then restart time to do the activities once I arrive.
- **If you could travel in time, would you go to the past or future? What year and why?** If I could go back in time, I would like to go back ten thousand years. It must be so interesting to see what the world looked like before human development. Or I would like to go one thousand years into the future to see what amazing technologies and differences there will be.
- **How many clocks are in your house? (Phone, watches and computers count too.)** I have two watches at home, one clock, and time on my phone and computer.
- **What time do you set your alarm in the mornings?** I set my alarm for 7:30 in the morning. That gives me some to wake up slowly.
- **What activity takes the most time of your life?** How much time does it take every week? For every human, the activity that takes up the most time is definitely sleep. Most people sleep around seven to eight hours a night. In a week I sleep around fifty hours a week.

9. **Can you describe your perfect day?** I wake up 7 am, I drink coffee and check the news. At 8 am I go to the gym and exercise for an hour. After that I go to work; I work from 9 am to noon. Lunch is from 12 to 1. Then from 1 to 5 pm I continue working. From 5 to 6 pm I go for a walk with my dog. In the evening I prepare dinner and from 8 to 10 relax with my family. I end my day by reading a book and falling asleep.

22 Books

QUESTIONS & ANSWERS STUDENT A

- **What is the last book you read?** The last book I've read was 'How to stop worrying and start living' by Dale Carnegie, whose most famous book 'How to make friends and influence friends' sold 30 million copies.
- **Did your parents read to you when you were young?** My dad used to read a lot of passages from the Bible that I learned many lessons from.
- **Is there a book that you have read more than once?** I can't remember if I read a book twice, but I thought about reading 'Lord of the Rings' by JRR Tolkien again.
- **Where can you get books?** These days most books are sold on the internet through Amazon or other online sites, or you can go to a bookstore to buy one.
- **Who is your favorite protagonist from a book?** One of my favorite protagonists is Mister Darcy from *'Pride and Prejudice'*. Throughout the book he is very stoic and serious, but we learn that he cares about the people close to him.
- **Which do you prefer: Audiobook, paperback, hardback or e-book?** An audiobook is a book you can listen to, paperback is when you have a foldable cover, hardback is when it has a hard cover and e-book is a book that you can read on an electronic device like a tablet or e-reader.
- **What book would you recommend to children?** I would recommend something like 'The Alchemist.' It's a book about a boy on a journey where he learns many lessons about life.
- **Why doesn't everyone enjoy reading?** Reading takes a lot of time and these days there are many other distractions that take up our time like phones and computers.
- **Can a book change the world?** The most published book by far is the Bible, it has shaped a lot of Western civilization.
- **If you could be any character in a book, who would it be?** In the classic novel 'Moby Dick' the main protagonist or character is called Ismail. He travels with the captain and crew in the search for Moby Dick (a legendary

giant whale). So, I would love to be this character, because he goes on an adventure and interacts with interesting characters.

Q&A - 22 BOOKS - STUDENT B

1. **What's your favorite book?** My favorite book is 'Great Expectations' by Charles Dickens. I read it when I was young and liked it because I learned a lot from the story. It is a difficult book to read so it helped improve my reading skills.
2. **Do you prefer fiction or non-fiction books?** Fiction means that it is made-up or fantasy, while non-fiction means that it deals in facts. When I was a teenager, I really enjoyed fantasy and fiction books, but now as an adult I prefer reading non-fiction or self-help books.
3. **How often do you read?** I read around a book a month. Whenever I drive or travel somewhere I listen to an audiobook. I find it very relaxing and a good use of my time.
4. **What's your favorite kind of book?** These days I enjoy self-help books about success and business. I want to learn new ideas that I can improve my life.
5. **If you could write a book, what would it be about?** If I could write a book, I would write a non-fiction book about teaching. I would include my journey as a teacher as well as research, great tips and techniques for teachers to use in the classroom.
6. **Can you name any famous authors?** There are many fantastic authors: Ernest Hemingway, Virginia Wolf, Jane Austin, William Shakespeare and Charles Dickens. Some current authors are James Patterson and Steven King.
7. **Why do many people say that books are better than movies?** When you read a book, you create the story using your imagination. Movies are made for a general audience, but in books you express your imagination.
8. **Most successful CEOs read 50 books a year but the average person only three. How can books help someone be more successful?** Reading books will gain you knowledge and stir up new ideas. Successful people like CEO's read lots of books then apply that to their businesses and lives.
9. **Is there a famous book from your country?** There is a famous book from South Africa called 'Cry the Beloved Country' by Alan Paton.

0. **Do you think books will disappear? How can that become a reality?** I believe that books won't disappear but the format of books might. We may have more e-books or audio books, but people will always love holding real books in their hands.

23 Sports

QUESTIONS & ANSWERS STUDENT A

1. **What are some sports that you enjoy watching?** I enjoy watching rugby, UFC (mixed martial-arts) and World Cup events.
2. **What sports are popular in your country?** In South Africa the most popular sports are rugby, cricket and soccer.
3. **What are some of the biggest sports events?** Every four years there is the football World Cup, rugby World Cup and cricket World Cup. Another four-year event is the Olympics; you get the summer and the winter Olympics. The United States has the Super Bowl for American football. For tennis lovers the major event is Wimbledon.
4. **The greatest players are called GOATs. Who are some GOATs that you know?** GOAT stands for 'Greatest of All Time', so when it comes to basketball, we see Michael Jordan as the GOAT; in cricket one of the GOATs would be Sasin Tendulkar. In football, contenders for GOAT-status are Renaldo and Messi.
5. **What do you think is the most dangerous sport?** There are many extreme and dangerous sports like racing events where, if an accident happens, you could die. I believe the most dangerous sport is boxing because of the number of knocks to the head have long-lasting effects.
6. **Some people are huge sports fans. Why do you think people become so emotional over sport?** In the past we had wars where groups fought against each other; we still have that instinct to support a team or a specific player. That is why fans are very emotional and passionate about their teams.
7. **What is a negative sports memory that you have?** When I was younger, I used to play rugby and the most negative sports memory I have is losing in a championship match.
8. **What are some benefits of playing sports?** When you practice a sport you get physical exercise, learn new skills and dedicate yourself to practice. In team sports you also learn social skills.
9. **Can you give some examples of extreme sports?** Extreme sports are like

skydiving, kayaking and free diving. They give a great adrenaline rush to the person doing it.

10. **What is good sportsmanship?** Good sportsmanship is to respect other competitors, officials and spectators and not to be vulgar in conduct, not to be a sore loser, but also not to be extremely boastful in victory.

Q&A - 23 SPORTS - STUDENT B

1. **What's your favorite sport to play?** My favorite sport is rugby. When I was younger I used to play rugby, these days I still enjoy playing touch rugby, which has no intense physical contact.
2. **Who is a famous sportsman/sportswoman from your country?** South Africa's famous golf players include Gary Player and Ernie Els; a famous cricketer is AB de Villiers. We also have many international rugby players.
3. **Do you have any favorite events at the Olympics?** I enjoy watching the summer Olympics, especially the big running events like the 100-meter dash or the 400 meters, also some field events like shot put and javelin.
4. **Do you think athletes are overpaid?** Athletes get paid for their physical attributes and unique skills. Because they have a short career and risk injury, many make a lot of money.
5. **Do you have a team that you support?** I love rugby, so I support the South African rugby team who coincidentally won the World Cup in 2019. My favorite local team is called the Cheetahs.
6. **What positive sport memory do you have?** When I was ten-year-old our rugby team won the provincial title. I was so proud and happy to be part of that group.
7. **Do you prefer individual or team sports?** Growing up, I mostly played team sports. Now as an adult, I regret not having spent more time on an individual events, so I can play it on my own.
8. **How do some people cheat at sports?** Some people cheat at sport by taking steroids to make themselves stronger; cheaters get caught and banned for using illegal substances.
9. **If you could be great at any sport, which would it be?** If I could be great at any sport, it would probably be football, because it is the most

supported sport. Also, there is more money to be made as a football player.

9. **John Wooden said: "Some believe sports build character. I believe that sports reveal character." What does that mean?** To be great at a sport you need to put in a lot of hard work; it takes character, commitment, talent and heart to get to the top of your sport.

24 Religion

QUESTIONS & ANSWERS STUDENT A

1. **Do you believe in God?** Yes, I believe in God. I believe that God created us and gave each of us a purpose. /No, I don't believe there is a god, I'm atheist.
2. **What are some of the major religions in the world?** There is Christianity, Buddhism, Islam, Hinduism and Judaism.
3. **Do you think religion is good or bad? What is good about religion?** My believe is that religion has caused a lot of good in the world, because it gave us order and laws to obey. Most religions teach us to be good and moral people.
4. **What are some religious holidays that you are aware of?** In Christianity there is Christmas and Easter; there are Hindu festivals such as Diwali and Holi; in Islam there are Al-Ishrat and Ramadan.
5. **Religions have rules or guidelines. What are some religious laws that you know about?** All religions have some rules about how we should behave, these laws have been passed on from ages ago and people still follow them today.
6. **Do you like talking about religion?** Religion is one of the most difficult topics to talk about. We always say that you should never talk about religion or politics, because there can easily be conflict between people with different beliefs.
7. **How does a religion start? Can you give an example?** Most religions start with a deity like a god and then there is a messenger. In the case of Christianity, Jesus came as explained in the Bible.
8. **Do you know anything about Jesus, Mohammed or Buddha?** I don't know the exact story, but Jesus, Buddha and Mohammed went through trials and began to share their message about God with people.
9. **Religion is a sensitive topic. Why do you think that is?** Different belief systems can bring people into conflict, so people of different religions should respect each other's beliefs.
10. **Do you think people that follow a religion are better than those who**

don't (atheists)? No, I don't think so. The way that you treat other people and the way that you behave show what kind of person you are. So, I do not think that those who follow a religion are necessarily better than those who don't.

Q&A - 24 RELIGION - STUDENT B

- **Do you pray?** Yes, I pray every night;/ Yes, I pray occasionally. /If I'm going through a difficult time, I pray to find salvation.
- **Some major religions are Christianity, Islam and Buddhism. What do they have in common?** Major religions like Christianity, Islam and Buddhism all have a God and a messenger as similarities.
- **Religion has caused some conflicts. What are some negative things about religion?** Religion is bad when non-believers are attacked for not following the same faith as the dominant religion.
- **Some people don't believe in a religion, they are called atheists. Why don't they believe in a god?** Most atheists believe that there is no scientific evidence for God or that any of the events happened.
- **How often do people go to church, mosque or a temple?** When I was young, I used to go to church every Sunday. Now I don't follow my religion as closely as I should and don't go to church often.
- **Every church has a leader or priest. How does one become a priest?** To become a priest, you need to intensively study the religious scripts of the particular faith and dedicate your life to it.
- **What do you think the world would be like without religion?** Religious laws have impacted the societies in which we live. It is also a way for us to reflect and be better people, so the world would be much different if it wasn't for religion.
- **What would Jesus, Mohammed or Buddha think about the world today?** I think they would be surprised or sad at what the world has become. We are meant to take care of the earth and each other, and in many aspects, we have failed to do that.
- **What religious practices do you think are strange to you?** I saw this one festival in India where many young people put hooks through their flesh; it was very strange and it looked painful.

). **Do you think religion can fit into our modern-day world?** Most religions preach prosperity and peace. Religion has a place in society even if things are constantly changing and technology is driving us ahead.

25 News

QUESTIONS & ANSWERS STUDENT A

- **What is some current news from your country?** South Korea has a sharp decrease in demographics. It means that more people are dying than being born, so the population is decreasing with less working people to pay taxes.
- **Where do you get your news?** In the past people got their news from newspapers, or watching television. These days however, most people go online to find news on websites or YouTube.
- **What is some good news that you have heard recently?** Recently I heard the news that vaccines will soon be released, which could mean that the Covid-19 pandemic will soon be over – fingers crossed.
- **Do you think there is too much politics in news?** Politics is important because politicians make decisions which affect our lives, so we have to know what is going on. However, all the news we get has some kind of bias as the media interpret the news in a way that suits their agenda.
- **Do you stay up to date with the news?** Yes, I follow general news, because it's important to be knowledgeable about what is happening around us. But most news won't affect our everyday lives.
- **Can you think of a headline for your country's newspaper tomorrow?** Headlines should be short, to the point and grab attention. So, my headline for the news would be: "Covid-19 could be crushed by 2023".
- **Many news platforms are being labeled as 'Fake News'. Do you think this is fair?** News has become very bias and is spun to suit their agendas. We have to read news from a variety of sources to get a fair assessment of what is happening.
- **What is the big news story in your life?** Currently my life is boring; I have no headlines at this moment so my news story could be: "Educator shoots 200th video."
- **Do you think the internet will kill traditional news like newspapers and TV?** Yes, most news networks have switched to reporting online as most people get up-to-date news off the internet. Newspapers are dying

out.
10. **If you were in the news, what would you want it to be for?** If I was in the news, I wish it was for helping English learners and teachers to be more successful in the classroom.

Q&A - 25 NEWS - STUDENT B

1. **What is some current international news?** The news everyone is talking about is Covid-19. We all are speculating when the pandemic will be over and what the lasting effects of this dark period in human history will be.
2. **What sources of news can you think of TV, radio etc.?** News sources are now online; you can search on Google, go to a news website or look on social media like Twitter. You can also get news from traditional media such as newspapers, TV and radio.
3. **Why is the majority of news negative?** The majority of news is negative because 'bad news sells!' Our attention is drawn to bad news therefore news companies are more eager to broadcast negative news – to get us watching.
4. **What kind of news stories interest you the most?** I'm interested in news stories that are different; people doing amazing things or inventing something to improve our lives.
5. **What different sections are there in the news?** You get the headlines, politics, sport and social news - gossip about celebrities. Then there is business news, classified advertisements, crime plus editorials by the editor and columnists.
6. **What is the most memorable news that you have ever seen?** I think for most people my age the most significant news event was the 9/11 terrorist attacks in New York. I was a teenager and watching TV when suddenly this report showed the airplanes crashing into the World Trade Center.
7. **Should news platforms give their opinion?** Of course, news will always be biased in some way because we see things through different lenses. So, make sure to look at other news sources too, because everything these days is filtered through an opinion.
8. **If the news reported about you last week, what would the headline be?** Last week I went on a short trip, so the headline would be: 'Eric's fun week away'.

8. **How would your life change without watching the news?** Honestly, I think less news is better than too much news. People are bombarded with news stories and their whole life revolves around what they see on social media and the internet.
9. **Would you ever get a job in the news industry?** No, but if did I would love to share information on education. It could be writing, or interviewing famous educators and scientists.

26 Money

QUESTIONS & ANSWERS STUDENT A

- **What is the last thing you bought?** That last thing I bought was a pack of razors. This afternoon I went grocery shopping; I bought tomato, lettuce, ham and razors.
- **What is your favorite shop?** For clothes I like a shop called 'Uniqlo', where I get most of my V-neck T-shirts. For food I enjoy going to 'Costco', where you can buy lots of great Western food and products at a good price. I tend to overspend on my budget whenever I go there.
- **Who is someone very rich?** The world's richest man is Jeff Bezos. He owns Amazon and many believe he will be the first person to be worth one thousand billion dollars.
- **How would you spend $20/ $200/ $2000?** With 20 dollars I would treat myself to a good meal. With 200 dollars I would go on a nice trip; rent a hotel and enjoy a weekend away. If I had 2,000 dollars, I would probably spend it on electronics, something like a new laptop.
- **How can you save money?** It is important to try and save money every month with your salary, put part of it, maybe ten percent, or twenty percent if it's possible, into a savings or investment account. That way you will consistently grow your savings and after a couple of years will be worth a lot more.
- **Do you give money to charity?** Sometimes I will send some money online to a charity. I do help out some friends and family members when they need money.
- **Do you think credit cards are good or bad?** It depends. If you use your credit card irresponsibly, you will go into debt. But if you use it in a smart way to collect points for the future and only use it appropriately, it can be a good thing.
- **What is the most money you've ever had on you?** The most money I ever had with me was ten thousand US dollars. I had to withdraw it from the bank to pay a deposit on an apartment and they wanted it in cash. I was very nervous walking around with so much money.

- **How did society function before money?** Before we started using money, people used bartering. Bartering is when you have a product and exchange it for something you need.
- **What type of taxes do you pay?** Every time you buy something you pay value added tax (VAT) and every time you receive a salary you pay income tax. There are many other types of taxes that you pay so the government can provide us the services we need to function.

Q&A - 26 MONEY - STUDENT B

- **Do you get (receive) a salary or allowance?** A salary is what you get monthly for a job you do; an allowance is something you receive from your parents. I receive a salary from the university I work at. When I was younger, I received an allowance from my parents.
- **What do you use money for?** We require money to live. We use money to pay for our housing, our food, transportation and entertainment. We need money to live and to get money we need to work.
- **How do rich people make money?** Rich people have assets that make them money; it could be property they rent out, a business that makes money, or investments.
- **Why do some people have money problems?** Most money problems come from overspending. If a person with a limited income constantly overspends it, they will fall into debt.
- **What is the most money that you have ever spent?** My biggest expense was buying a car. In the future I would like to buy a house and that would probably be the most money I would ever spend.
- **Can money buy happiness?** No, money cannot buy happiness, but it can buy you freedom and options. You do need money otherwise it will be another problem that makes you unhappy.
- **Have you ever lost money?** No, I haven't lost a lot of money, but I feel like I've spent or wasted a lot of money over the years.
- **How can you earn more money?** You have to build assets that can make you money. It could be by creating products; starting a business; buying property, or investing intelligently. It is very difficult, which is why only a small percentage of people get rich.
- **How would you live your life if you were mega rich?** I want to live in a

big house near the beach with a beautiful view while doing hobbies that I really enjoy.

9. **Do you think money can buy love?** No, there are lots of rich people without love and many poor people with love. So, money cannot buy happiness, but it does give you an advantage – I guess.

27 Parties

QUESTIONS & ANSWERS STUDENT A

- **What is the last party you went to?** A: One of my friends celebrated his baby's first 100 days. In Korea parents hold a big party when a baby turns 100 days old. I took a small gift.
- **What do you like to do at parties?** Parties are meant to be social, so I like meeting new people and chatting with them. I also like playing games like darts, dancing and having a good time.
- **What type of parties do you know of?** There are birthday parties, anniversaries, New Year's Eve parties, or just a party organized to get people together.
- **Should you take gifts to a party?** Gifts are not always required, unless it's a birthday party, but taking something for the host is a good idea.
- **What makes a good host for a party?** A good host prepares everything: the music, food and atmosphere where guests can have a good time. The also take the effort to introduce people to one another. A host's job is not easy, so we should appreciate them.
- **What games or activities to you play at parties?** Any icebreaker is good way to start a party because most people are nervous when they first arrive. By playing an icebreaker you create a welcoming atmosphere and help guests to relax.
- **What does RSVP mean?** RSVP is French for 'repondez, s'il vous plaît,' which means 'respond please'. You have to let the host know if you will attend and bring a partner.
- **What is the best party you've ever been to?** My favorite type of parties are the ones where you dress up in costumes, so I am a big fan of Halloween.
- **What can go wrong at a party?** There could be problems with the music, or the weather could impact it's held outside. It is also bad if there isn't enough food or drinks for the guests.
- **If you could invite any celebrity to your party, who would it be?** If I could invite any celebrity, I'd invite Ryan Reynolds from Deadpool. He

has a great sense of humor so people will enjoy talking to him.

27 Q&A STUDENT B

1. **What is the last party you hosted?** A couple of weeks ago I invited some friends to come to my apartment and play boardgames. We had a good time eating pizza, making jokes and playing board games.
2. **What kind of food can you serve at a party?** It depends on what kind of party it is. If it is a wedding reception, people expect a full meal. If it is just a regular party with drinks, it is a good idea to have snacks or finger food. Make sure to let the guests know what to expect ahead of time.
3. **How are people invited to parties?** The traditional way of inviting someone to a party is to give an invitation. These days we invite everyone via a group chat.
4. **What is a good excuse to give if you can't go to a party**? If you can't go to a party you can simply thank the host for the invitation and tell them that you already have other plans.
5. **What do you need to have a good party?** You need a good atmosphere, food and drinks, music, enough space and a bathroom for everyone.
6. **What are some parties that you have specific to your country?** In South Africa we have Heritage Day on September 24th, we also refer to it as Braai Day. Braai is the word we use in South Africa for barbeque.
7. **Did you ever have dance parties at your high school?** In middle and high school we have formal dances where boys and girls would dance together.
8. **What party games do you know?** I like games like Charades where you have to act out scenarios. Group games are a lot of fun.
9. **Have you ever had a bad experience at a party?** Once at a party, I got very sick. I really wanted to stay, but I didn't feel well so decided that it would be better to leave.
10. **If you could host any type of party in the future, what kind of party would it be?** If I could host any party, I would host a post-Covid party. Everyone will celebrate the end of the pandemic and live life freely.

28 Goals

QUESTIONS & ANSWERS STUDENT A

- **What are your goals for the future?** In the future I would like to shoot many videos to help teachers and students. I also want to get married and start a family.
- **Why is it important to write down your goals?** When you write down your goals you are putting it on paper, making it real. When someone doesn't write down their goals, it stays an idea within their heads. Writing gives you a kind of map to follow to reach your dreams.
- **What are your career goals?** In the next five years I hope to give some talks on education; learn more about how to be a better teacher and then to pursue a doctorate, a PhD in education.
- **Does your family have goals?** As a family we grew up to be God-fearing and honest people. We also aim to be a benefit to our community.
- **Have you ever failed or given up on a goal?** Sometimes we pursue short term goals that evolve and change into something new. When I was young, I thought that I could teach one year in every country I like; since then, my goals have become more realistic.
- **What is something you never learned but wish you did?** I wish I learned how to play a musical instrument when I was younger. Write down your goals and do something every day that moves you closer to that goal. Plan for success and move in that direction.
- **What can you do now to be successful in the future?** Write down your goals and do something every day that moves you closer to that goal. Plan for success and move in that direction.
- **Do you think money and fame equals success?** Your success depends on the goals that you have for your life. Achieving your goals and finding happiness is success. From the outside we believe that rich and famous people have succeeded in life, but that may not be true.
- **How do you motivate yourself to achieve your goals?** There is a famous expression of burning your boats. The only choice for me is to move forward and achieve those goals. We need this mental attitude of always

pushing forward to go for what we want in life.

). **What is the difference between a goal and a dream?** A dream is an idea or a hope you have for the future. A goal is something you set for yourself and you take steps to achieve: Make it realistic, spend time on a plan then work hard to achieve your goal.

28 Q & A STUDENT B

- **What do you want to achieve this week?** This week I plan on filming at least forty videos in this video series. It is very difficult and right now I am at 28 videos, I need twelve before the end of the week to feel content.
- **Should parents help their children set goals?** Definitely. Parents need to teach their children how to set goals for what they want to achieve in life.
- **What are your educational goals?** My educational goal is to improve as a teacher; to learn more about pedagogy and educational theory. So, this year I'll learn more about teaching, I'll shoot videos and also spend time working on my Korean.
- **Which goals are the most important?** Personal, physical, financial, career or education? Well, it depends on what is most important to you. Do you want to improve your career, education or finances? It all depends on what you want from life to feel successful.
- **Do men and women have different goals?** Men and women have different goals; just like every individual has unique goals because we have different values and needs.
- **Many people have a 5-year plan. What is yours?** My five-year plan is to work hard on my YouTube channel and career. I would also like to get married, but order to do that I need to meet the 'right' someone.
- **Who is the most successful person in your family? Why?** I have an uncle who made a success in business through hard work and determination.
- **Can you tell me about a goal that you've achieved in your life?** Well, I had the goal to become a teacher and eventually one day work at a university. So, I studied hard and I got the necessary experience. Eventually I achieved my goal of working as a teacher at a university.
- **Do you think goals change between countries?** Every country wants

success and happiness for its people, but each one is different and has to do its best to succeed.

10. **Who can help you achieve your goals?** Achieving your goals is up to you, but people like your family, friends and colleagues can help you. You can also find a mentor and coach to support you.

29 Technology

QUESTIONS & ANSWERS STUDENT A

1. **What technology do you use in your daily life?** I use my mobile phone and laptop hundreds of times a day. Most people rely heavily on their phones for entertainment, communication and access to information.
2. **What technology has improved the most in the past decade (10 years)?** In the past ten years the internet has improved the most. It's faster and easier to use than before making it accessible to more people around the world.
3. **How has technology affected travel?** When I was young, we had to open up maps to find the correct route, but these days everyone uses a GPS. Technology in the future will have self-driving cars taking it even a step further.
4. **Who in your family knows the most about new technology? (Who is an early adopter?)** And early adopter is someone who gets onto a new technological trend quicker. Most people wait for a new device to be widely used before they try it, but an early adopter wants it first.
5. **How has technology changed learning?** Most learning was forced online with lectures conducted by video on computers. We can expect education to evolve as technology improves and see more virtual reality learning in the future.
6. **What problems come with better technology?** Unfortunately, we are losing our ability to communicate without technology. It is more difficult for us to connect and stay engaged when we are face-to-face with other people.
7. **How has technology changed your life compared to the lives of your parents?** I think my parent's generation was isolated from the world. No, I can get information quickly. If I need to contact someone I can do so very easily. They had to rely on their own.
8. **Do you wish you could take a break from technology?** What would you do or where would you go? Yes, I believe we should take short breaks from technology. For example, I don't take my phone with me when I go

to the gym.
9. **If you could work on any technology, what would it be?** I would like to learn more about educational technology; how to connect and best prepare learners in the future.
10. **If you had children, how would you teach them about technology?** I would limit my children on how much technology they use; I would encourage them to spend time away from electronic devices.

29 Q&A STUDENT B

1. **What technology can't you live without?** I can't live without my phone because I rely on it to do so many things: To communicate with friends, to look up information and to stay entertained – but I'm not sure if it's good for society.
2. **What technology do you expect to see in the next 10 years?** I expect to see driverless cars, where people can get into a car and it will drive by itself. Also, I think there will be a way so that information can travel quicker between our brain and the technology. It is scary but also interesting.
3. **How has technology affected communication?** Communication has improved by leaps and bounds. Now it is so easy to connect through the internet: by calling, messaging and video.
4. **Why is it more difficult for older people to adapt to new technology?** Humans like stability, so as you get older it gets more difficult to learn new things.
5. **How has technology made your life easier?** Technology is always expanding and influences the way we live. It has improved the way we connect with friends on social media, get news, do mobile banking and study. All without needing to leave our homes.
6. **Do you trust technology? What dangers are there with technology?** With more of our information online, we have to be mindful of its security. If the wrong person gets their hands on it, it could cost you dearly.
7. **How did technology change your parents' lives from your grandparents' lives?** During my parents' lives more people had access to telephones than in the days of our grandparents. Television also became

mainstream.
7. **How do you entertain yourself with technology?** I watch videos, check friends on Instagram or Facebook, read things online and occasionally play computer games.
8. **What technology do you think the world needs to focus on right now?** A lot of technology is moving into green technology where we try to reduce pollution and improve the environment.
9. **Which technology do you think has been the most important to civilization?** The most important technology developed in history was probably the electric light. When it became broadly used, people could see better at night and thus work longer hours. That productivity helped us evolve faster as a society.

30 Problems

QUESTIONS & ANSWERS STUDENT A

- **How do you relax at home?** I relax at home by lying on my bed and watching Netflix on my laptop. While I do this, I check my phone and chat to my friends.
- **What is a problem that is bothering you right now?** Right now, the frame of my bed is broken so I need to buy a new one and get rid of the old.
- **Who do you ask for advice about your problems?** If I have problems with my work or relationships, I often video chat with a friend to talk about it. Even if I don't follow his advice, I feel better by just talking about my problems.
- **Are you a creative problem solver**? Yes, I think I solve problems by seeking unique solutions.
- **Do you like staying busy? Why?** Yes, I like staying busy so I create many projects that I try to finish. It keeps me focused. If I don't have something to do – a project, or something to pursue with purpose, then I don't feel happy.
- **What's the best life advice that you've heard?** The best advice I have received was when my dad convinced me to study education and then encouraged me to teach in Korea.
- **Have you ever helped a stranger?** Whenever I am in a situation where I can help a stranger in a difficult situation, I try to help them.
- **Are there specific situations that you find stressful?** I get stressed whenever I'm late for a meeting or unprepared for a presentation, so the best I can do is to arrive early and also to be prepared for whatever I have to do.
- **What problems do your parents struggle with?** I love my parents but they are stubborn and don't like to try new things. I have to persuade them to try new food or do anything different.
- **If you could give advice to yourself from five years ago, what would it be?** If I could go back five years, I would tell myself just to go for it,

because waiting is way worse than whatever problems you might encounter.

30 Q&A STUDENT B

- **Do you lead a stressful life?** No, I don't have a stressful life. Compared to other people in the world my life is relatively stress-free, so I should count myself lucky.
- **What is a problem that you've recently overcome?** I recently sat down for 30 minutes and figured out how to use some Korean apps on my phone to order goods online.
- **Do your friends come to you for advice? How do you help them?** When people come to me with their problems, I ask them: Do you want advice, or do you just need someone to listen. We often get into the habit of giving advice when a friend probably only wants a kind ear to listen.
- **How do you cope with stress?** Whenever I have stress I go for a walk, exercise, or I take ten minutes to meditate. Try to stay in the moment to let go of worries.
- **What doesn't kill you makes you stronger. Do you agree?** When you go through something difficult you have to learn from it. Why did it happened and also how you can prevent it from happening again in the future.
- **What work takes up most of your time and energy?** The work that takes up most of my energy is my procrastination! I spend too much of my time trying to get the energy to do something, to work on a project, to exercise or to face my responsibilities.

- **Anxiety and depression are big issues in the modern world. Do you sometimes struggle with it?** On social media we see people talking about anxiety and depression. We should tell them it's okay to be anxious and depressed, but that's not the way you want to be, you want to be in a positive and relaxed state.
- **How can you fix one of your problems?** I think the majority of problems can be fixed by facing it head on. I write down what the problem is and what steps I need to take in order to solve it. Finally, I take action to

resolve it.

8. **What problems do your grandparents struggle with?** My grandparents lived during a world war, before a time of television and phones. In comparison to them I'm living a life of luxury.

9. **Which would you choose: A stressful job with a high salary or a low paying job with zero stress?** I would actually prefer a high stress job with a high salary for a short amount of time, because a low-paying job with zero stress means that you are not improving. We need some stress in our lives to improve.

31 Accidents

QUESTIONS & ANSWERS STUDENT A

1. **Have you ever broken a bone?** No, I've been lucky not to have broken a bone. / Yes, I've broken my arm. While I was running down the stairs, I tripped, fell and broke my arm. My mom took me to the hospital where they put on a cast.
2. **What do firefighters do?** Firefighters help us in case of emergencies. For example, when there is a fire, they quickly put on their protective gear and rush to put it out. If there is some kind of accident; if someone is stuck in a car wreck or elevator, they have the right equipment to deal with most emergencies.
3. **What is the most dangerous thing in your kitchen?** The most dangerous things in a kitchen are usually knives and the stove. You have to be very careful when you cut with a knife or when you use the stove. Always switch off the gas when you are not using it.
4. **Have you trained in first aid?** Yes, I have taken first aid training before. As a teacher you are required to receive first aid training. It's very helpful if an accident happens so you know what steps to take.
5. **How can we prevent accidents?** Give an example. We can minimize the chance of an accident happening by taking precautions, for example: to cover sharp edges on furniture with some kind of plastic. You can also babyproof your house by locking cabinets that contain dangerous chemicals.
6. **Do you often worry about getting into an accident?** I am very careful not to get into an accident when I drive; I make sure to pay attention to the road and drive under the speed limit.
7. **Have you or your parents ever filed an insurance claim?** Insurance is something you pay every month in case something breaks or gets stolen.
8. **Have you ever been admitted to hospital?** (If you haven't, then share an experience about visiting the hospital.) I have only been admitted to a hospital for tonsilitis – to remove my tonsils – when I was very young. Besides that, I have never been admitted into a hospital.

9. **What's a tragic story that you saw in the news?** Yesterday I saw a story in the news of a young man who had a car accident which caused very bad burns all over his body. I felt really bad for him.
10. **What should you do in case of a fire?** If the fire gets out of control and you can't put it out yourself, immediately call the fire department and get outside of your house as quickly as possible.

Q&A- 31 ACCIDENTS - STUDENT B

1. **Have you ever been in or seen a car accident?** I've been in a car accident only once. A friend was driving and bumped his car over a pavement. The car took a lot of damage, but nobody got hurt.
2. **Have you ever made an emergency call?** No, I've never made an emergency call. / Yes, I've had to call the police before. My shoes got stolen, so I called the police.
3. **What dangers can be found in a bathroom that could cause an accident?** Bathrooms can get very slippery, so someone can easily slip and fall. Some people leave medicine in the bathroom that could be accessible to children.
4. **Do you know anybody that is accident prone?** Accident prone means to get into many accidents. Recently I thought I was kind of accident prone; because I hurt my knee a couple of weeks ago, then I cut my hand and needed stitches and a week after that I had an eye infection. Fortunately, I'm all better now.
5. **Have you ever helped someone who had an accident?** Yes, someone was feeling really bad and I had to drive them to the emergency room to see a doctor.
6. **What kind of training can you get to prepare for an emergency?** First Aid is the main type of training that you can get to prepare for accidents. You learn what to do in case someone has an accident to help them if there isn't a doctor nearby.
7. **What do your parents warn you about before you go out?** My parents warned me to stay safe and check all my belongings when walking down the street or going to a party. They also tell me to dress warm if it's cold outside.
8. **Have you ever visited someone at a hospital?** Yes, I've visited many

people in the hospital. When they are sick or getting surgery, I visit them and take them a gift to cheer them up. It can get very boring when you are all alone at hospital, so I visit them often.

8. **What big tragedy happened in the last ten years?** Recently there was a flight from Indonesia that crashed close to Djakarta and many people died. It is such a tragedy when lives are lost.

9. **What should you do in case of an earthquake?** Earthquakes are measured in the Richter scale. Big earthquakes can cause buildings to collapse and you need to get away from the building so that no debris falls on you.

32 Work and Jobs

QUESTIONS & ANSWERS STUDENT A

- **What job do you want to do in the future?** In the future I would like to be an engineer.
- **What is one of the most exciting jobs you can think of?** I think a race car driver is a job that must be very exciting. It can be dangerous, but an adrenaline rush because of the speed.
- **Are you a hard worker AND what motivates you?** Yes, I think I'm a hard worker. I always complete my tasks on time and I really push myself to deliver the best work possible. My salary at the end of the month motivates me! No, what really motivates me is doing a good job and learning new skills that will help me become a better teacher in the future.
- **What professions are well-paid these days?** Doctor, Lawyer etc. Occupations where someone specializes in a specific field, such as doctors and lawyers, always get paid well. So too people who work in a STEM related job. (STEM is science, technology, engineering and mathematics.)
- **Would you like to work in another country?** Currently I'm working in another country, but I would like to travel and work in many other countries before I retire.
- **Is it possible to become a millionaire by only working a normal job?** It depends what job you have and how much your salary is, then you can save and eventually become a millionaire. But in reality, most people become millionaires by investing their money, buying property or starting a business.
- **At what age would you like to retire?** I would like to retire when I'm around seventy so that I have enough time to enjoy the last decades of my life.
- **Have you had a job interview and how did it go?** Most of my interviews go well. I try to appear confident and answer their questions as well as I possibly can. It is also important to present yourself as a capable person for the position.
- **Do you get along with your colleagues or other people if you do**

groupwork? Sometimes I get along with colleagues and we can work together; other times there is conflict because we have different ideas on the project. But, even if you don't get along with someone, we should try to work together to achieve our goals.

). **Do you know anyone who was fired from a job and why were they fired?** Yes, another professor was fired because she broke some rules and were often late for class. First, she received a warning and when she continued breaking rules, was eventually let go.

Q&A - 32 WORK AND JOBS - STUDENT B

- **What does your dad do for a living?** My dad has had many jobs. At first, he started as a journalist, then worked in public relations, in HR at a mine company and ended by teaching English.
- **What is the worst job you can think of?** I would hate to be stuck in an office cubicle. I prefer moving around and working with other people.
- **Is it easy to get a job in your country?** It depends, there are many low-paying jobs that anyone can do. But if you are looking for a high-paying specialist job, it will be more difficult.
- **Do people work long hours in your country?** I currently live in South Korea where people work very long hours. In most countries the normal workhours are from 9am to 5pm.
- **What is most important when choosing a job: Salary, enjoyment or freedom?** I think enjoyment is important, because then you love what you are doing and it doesn't feel like work. Salary is also important because money gives us freedom.
- **What would you do if you were unemployed?** If I was unemployed, I would be very stressed and apply for a job everywhere. As adults we need an income to survive.
- **Would you like to work for a company or start your own business?** It is much easier to work for a big company or organization than to start a business from scratch. More than 80% of small businesses do not survive for many years and they take a lot of effort manage.
- **What degree or experience do you need to get the job you want?** I would need more teaching experience, a PhD and do research to get the job I really want.

1. **What makes a good boss?** A good boss is someone that motivates you and clearly shows you how to achieve the goals they set out for you. A good boss is someone who allows you to grow and pushes you to be the best employee you can be.
2. **Do you think that a person's job determines their value?** Every job is unique and shapes the person doing it. Your experiences at your work will have an impact on who you are as a person.

33 Love

QUESTIONS & ANSWERS STUDENT A

- **Have you ever been in love?** Yes, I have been in love before. When I was young, I had a crush on a girl at school. I hope in the future to meet someone I really like and fall in love again.
- **There are different types of love?** Can you think of different examples of love? Yes, there are many different ways that we can love. There is romantic love, love between family and spiritual love.
- **What special days are there for people in love?** The most commonly known day for people in love is Valentine's Day on February 14th. Besides Valentine's Day there is also White Day in Asia on March 14th.
- **Do you believe in love at first sight?** Yes, I believe in love at first sight, when you see someone and feel immensely attracted to that person. Finding someone that is physically pretty or handsome is a start, but after that you should get to know them as a person to see if they suit you.
- **What is your favorite romance movie?** My favorite romance movie is 'Love Actually'. It is a popular romance movie often watched around Christmas.
- **Who do you think is more romantic, men or women?** I think both men and women are romantic but in different ways. As a man, I try to be romantic by doing things for a girl I like, whereas women have a deeper understanding about how to be romantic in the relationship.
- **What can you do to be more attractive to the opposite sex?** Obviously, you can work on your appearance by exercising and eating better; on your sense of fashion and your social skills, how to interact with people. You should also have a full life and having money also doesn't hurt.
- **Have you ever heard the expression: "There are many fish in the sea." Do you agree?** Yes, I think it is true. We get caught up in thinking that there is only one perfect person for us, but there are actually many other people that could potentially be great partners.
- **Why are people getting married and having children later in life?** These days we have many other things going on in our lives, so many

young people are waiting until much later to get married and have children.

9. **What are the benefits of remaining single?** If you remain single, you have more freedom to do as you please; you can be selfish with your time, money and energy. Unfortunately, you will also miss out on the feeling of having a family.

Q&A - 33 LOVE - STUDENT B

1. **Who is your celebrity crush?** My celebrity crush is Blake Lively. Unfortunately, she is already married to Ryan Reynolds, so I don't stand a chance.
2. **Is it possible to fall out of love? Why?** I am not a love doctor, so I'm not sure. But I believe that it is possible to fall out of love. One of the sad truths of the modern world is that more and more people are falling out of love and breaking up.
3. **What is a good gift for a boyfriend (bf) or girlfriend (gf)?** For a boyfriend, find out what he needs and buy that for him. For a girlfriend find out what she would like and buy that, but keep the receipt so that if you make a mistake – which most men do – she can return it for something else.
4. **Are you dating anyone right now?** No, at the moment I'm not seeing anyone, but if you know anyone that would suit me – introduce me!
5. **What is your favorite love song?** What's my favorite love song? I don't know. Maybe that Barry White song 'My darling, I can't get enough of your loving.'
6. **What is most important thing to you when choosing a bf/gf?** I guess I look for someone who also interested in me, who does things to show that they care about me, that pays attention to my needs and also someone that I enjoy spending time with.
7. **Do you believe in 'The One' or are there many possible spouses out there for a person?** No, I don't believe in 'The One'. There are millions of people in the world and you could potentially form a great relationship with several of them.
8. **How has dating changed in the modern world?** These days many people use apps to find a potential partner; Bumble, Tinder and similar

other apps to connect to someone and chat with them. Social media also has a great impact on the modern dating scene.
8. **Can you describe your perfect date?** My perfect date is going somewhere fun for an adventure so that you can enjoy the experience together.
9. **What difficulties are there in dating someone from another culture?** People are generally the same, but cultures differ towards dating, the way you interact with each other and show affection. Having similar values will make it more realistic for your relationship to last longer.

34 Food

QUESTIONS & ANSWERS STUDENT A

- **What is your favorite food?** My favorite food is my mom's food. /My favorite food is Italian food because I love eating pizza, spaghetti and risotto.
- **What are some famous foods from your country?** I am from South Africa which has great cuisine. One famous dish is bunny chow. Bunny chow is when they take a half-loaf of bread, hollow out the inside and insert a curry dish. It's delicious.
- **What fruits do you eat most often?** Out of all the fruits, I eat banana the most. Other fruits I enjoy are strawberries and apples.
- **Who cooks or prepares your food?** I usually go to a cafeteria or restaurant where the chef prepares the food. Sometimes I cook at home.
- **What is a vegetarian and why do people eat that way?** These days many people are vegetarian. Vegetarians don't eat meat because they consider it cruel to kill animals and find it healthier.
- **Do you have any food allergies?** I have a shellfish allergy; if I eat it, my face swells up and turns red.
- **How expensive is food in your country?** Right now, I live in South Korea where food is quite expensive, especially the price of fruit, meat and vegetables compared to other countries.
- **What special foods do you eat on holidays?** (Like Christmas for example.) I like to celebrate Thanksgiving with my American friends by eating turkey. On Christmas we enjoy roasted chicken; a family tradition.
- **What vegetables do you enjoy?** I enjoy all vegetables, which is very healthy. My favorite vegetable is broccoli, especially if you add a cheese sauce to it.
- **How does the etiquette of eating together differ from your country to other countries?** Most countries follow a similar etiquette when it comes to food with some minor differences. In South Africa it's normal to go to a restaurant by yourself, but in Korea eating is a social event where people eat with friends whenever possible.

Q&A - 34 FOOD - STUDENT B

1. **If you could only eat one food for the rest of your life, what would it be?** If I could only eat one food for the rest of my life, I would pick a burger. It has bread, meat, and vegetables like lettuce, onions, tomato and cheese.
2. **What food do you dislike?** There are a few foods that I don't enjoy. I especially dislike offal or organs like kidneys or liver. In some countries it is a delicacy, but I dislike eating animal organs.
3. **What toppings do you enjoy on your pizza?** I like a meaty pizza with some peperoni, ham, mushrooms and olives. And I don't mind pineapple on pizza. Many people dislike pineapple on their pizza, but I occasionally enjoy it.
4. **Are you a good cook?** I am definitely not a good cook although I'm trying to improve my skills. When I was young everyone around me cooked and I never bothered to learn. I am able to make simple dishes, but I still have a lot to learn.
5. **Are you concerned about your calorie intake when choosing a meal?** It's important to consider what we put into our bodies. Don't overeat and binge on unhealthy foods, but also don't obsess about it.
6. **What other country's food do you enjoy?** I actually enjoy Middle Eastern food a lot because they use a lot of lamb and a variety of spices.
7. **Do you often eat out? Where?** Yes, I often eat out. There are specific Korean and Western restaurants I visit regularly. For lunch I eat at the university cafeteria.
8. **What foods do you consider healthy?** I consider foods like vegetables, fruit, lean meat, nuts and grains as healthy. Sugary foods like donuts, bread and sweets are definitely unhealthy.
9. **Does your family have any recipes that are passed down from generation to generation?** Yes, my grandmother used to make the best milk tart, a South African dessert. Before she passed away, she gave the recipe to my mom to continue the tradition.
10. **What do you like for dessert after a meal?** I enjoy some sweet cakes such as tiramisu, sponge cake, or perhaps some chocolate ice-cream for dessert after a meal.

35 First times

QUESTIONS & ANSWERS STUDENT A

1. **What is the first thing you do when you wake up in the morning?** The first thing I do is check social media on my phone. Many people say that is a bad habit, but it's difficult to change.
2. **What was your first pet?** My first pet was a dog called Lion. She was gentle Staffordshire Terrier and had a lot of puppies.
3. **When is the first time you went to the cinema?** The first movie I remember watching in a cinema was 'The Little Mermaid'. I was around five or six years old and watched it with popcorn and cola.
4. **When is the first time you traveled alone?** I remember traveling eight hours on a bus to my grandmother's house one summer. It was very exciting and I enjoyed the snacks they served.
5. **When is the first time you bought a present for someone?** Buying presents is kind of difficult because you want to get something good. My first experience buying a gift was when I bought a chocolate on Valentine's Day.
6. **When is the first time you earned some money?** When I was young, I helped my cousin deliver newspapers and I received some money for that. Doing work to earn money is a good feeling.
7. **Tell me about your first boyfriend or girlfriend?** My first girlfriend was in elementary school and that relationship lasted about two days.
8. **What is the first country you traveled to?** If you haven't, what is the first country you would like to travel to? There is a small country called Lesotho on the inside of South Africa. One winter my brothers and I went to uncle's farm in Lesotho.
9. **What is the first dish you learned to cook?** The first thing I learned to cook was scrambled eggs. It was an accident, I wanted to make an omelet but messed it up.
10. **Where did you go the first time you flew on a plane?** The first time I flew on an airplane I was 25 years old and I traveled from South Africa to South Korea. The trip lasted 18 hours.

Q&A - 35 FIRST TIMES - STUDENT B

- **Who was the first person you talked to today?** One of my friends called me this morning. He is in quarantine and asked me to take him some supplies.
- **What happened the first time you got into trouble at school?** I got into trouble at school for fighting. I had to go to the principal's office and we were punished.
- **When is the first time you fell in love?** Falling in love is a very human emotion; when I was very young – maybe twelve years old – I fell in love with a girl, but nothing came out of it.
- **When is the first time that you bought something expensive?** The first expensive thing I bought was a car. It wasn't an expensive car but it was the most money I had spent at one time.
- **What is the first cellphone you ever owned?** I only received my first cellphone when I was seventeen old. It was called the Sagem SX, not a popular brand but I liked it nonetheless.
- **When is the first time you met your best friend?** I met my best friend at a party. We had a lot in common and spent more time together.
- **Why did you go to a hospital for the first time?** As a little boy I had my tonsils removed at hospital. After surgery, I was very confused but got to eat a lot of ice cream.
- **When did you first learn to swim?** I had swimming lessons when I was very young. My family enjoys going to the beach so I learned to swim from a young age.
- **When is the first time you lost something?** I remember going to a nearby shop to play some games but didn't lock my bicycle. When I returned, it was gone.
- **When is the first time you drank alcohol?** I drank a beer for the first time when I was 18. It was at a barbeque with friends.

36 If you could

QUESTIONS & ANSWERS STUDENT A

- **If you had one wish, what would it be?** Most people would wish for world peace, because then everyone would be safe and happy.
- **If you could be a celebrity for a day, who would it be?** I would like to be a celebrity that is respected by my peers and liked by my fans. So, I would like to be Brad Pitt.
- **If you were stranded on a deserted island, what would you take with you? If** there is electricity on the island, I would take my phone. But if there is no wi-fi; I would take a hunting knife to cut things and start fires.
- **If you had a superpower, what would it be?** I would like to be able to manipulate objects, that means that I can change any material around me.
- **If you could change anything in the past, what would it be?** I wouldn't be the person I am today if I changed something in the past. So I wouldn't change anything.
- **If you could buy a car right now, what car would it be?** I don't know a lot about cars, but if I could buy any car, it would be an expensive sportscar like a Ferrari.
- **If you could meet any historical figure, who would it be?** If I could meet any historical figure it would be Leonardo DaVinci. He was responsible for magnificent paintings, sculptures and ideas.
- **If you could know anything that happens in the future, what would it be?** I would collect sports betting results and investing tips. Then return and use that information to become rich.
- **If you could live in any TV show, which one would it be?** If I could live in any TV show, it would be in the world of Pokémon, where I could catch Pokémon and train them. That would be a lot of fun!
- **If you could do anything you want to, what would it be?** I would like to go to other countries to see and experience new things. I wish I could travel. At the moment nobody is able to travel freely, so I would love to travel

Q&A - 36 IF YOU COULD - STUDENT B

- **If you were rich, what would you do with the money?** If I was rich, I would buy a house next to the beach; get an expensive car, have a family with some pets. I will do everything I like and enjoy life.
- **If you could go anywhere in the world, where would you go?** There are so many places I wish to travel to, but these days I'm kind of curious about the Mediterranean.
- **If you could change one thing about yourself, what would it be?** My personality? No, if I could change one thing about myself, I wish I was braver, I wish I took more risks.
- **If you could pick a costume for Halloween, what would it be?** I really enjoy dressing up for Halloween. I usually like some kind of animated character. Next Halloween I might dress up as Kakashi from Naruto.
- **If you could change anything about your country, what would you change?** I'm from South Africa and if I could change anything in my country, I would like to solve the problems of corruption and crime.
- **If you could have an unlimited supply of one thing, what would it be?** I would want an unlimited supply of water. If any area has a drought, I could supply them with water.
- **If you could learn any skill, what would it be?** If I could learn any skill, it would be to improve my cooking or speak another language.
- **If you could live in any period of history, when would it be?** If I could go to any time in history, it would be the 1950's or 60's. Life was much simpler with less technology.
- **If you could stay one age forever, what age would that be?** I believe that the best age is around thirty because you have the benefit of youth and also wisdom that comes with experience.
- **If you were born in another country, which country would it be?** If I could have been born in any other country, I would like it to be Switzerland. Switzerland is a beautiful and fairly rich country, so chances are good that you could lead a good life.

37 Culture

QUESTIONS & ANSWERS STUDENT A

- **What do you think is something unique or interesting about your culture? In** South Africa, most white and indigenous brown people speak a language called Afrikaans, which evolved from Dutch.
- **What is considered rude in your culture?** Just like most cultures we show respect to other people when we meet; you smile when you greet them.
- **Do you know what culture shock is?** Culture shock is when you encounter a different culture from your own, where it is very different and something new to understand. For example, when I came to Korea, I experienced culture shock.
- **Is there anything that confuses you about another culture?** Sometimes when I see how people live in different countries, I take a step back and try to understand why they do things that way. Sometimes it is very difficult to agree with a culture that is so far different from your own.
- **What is some advice you would give to someone from your culture before traveling abroad?** The advice I would give to other South Africans is to try new and different things with an open mind and not automatically disregard it.
- **What single person has had the greatest influence on your culture?** The first European to colonize South Africa was called Jan van Riebeeck. He has had the greatest influence on my culture.
- **On what occasions do you give flowers in your culture?** We give flowers on special days like Valentine's Day, or someone's birthday. Oh, and don't forget Mother's Day.
- **What is the most important thing your culture has given the world?** My culture has great food and also meat products like boerewors which is a sausage and biltong; dried, cured meat.
- **Are tips at restaurants common?** What is a reasonable tip? In South Africa we give a 10% tip to waiters on the bill. For example, if the food cost $100, we would give a $10 tip. In South Korea though we don't leave

a tip at restaurants.
). **Is your country multicultural?** Is multiculturalism a good thing? Yes, South Africa is very multi-cultural. I believe it is a good thing because we learn from each other to improve as human beings.

Q&A - 37 CULTURE - STUDENT B

- **When people from other countries think about yours, what is the first thing they think about?** When people think of South Africa they might think about Nelson Mandela as a previous president; or they might think of apartheid, which was a policy where white and black people were separated.
- **What is something you admire from another country?** When I see people from other countries, for example the United States, Canada or European countries, I admire their confidence when traveling abroad.
- **What is something you would like to change about your culture?** I love my culture but I wish people were less stubborn about change and trying new things.
- **Is it polite to be straightforward and direct with anyone in your culture?** In South Korea you cannot be direct or speak plainly with someone of a higher position or older than you. You have to speak in a polite manner.
- **What is the best advice you can give to travelers coming to your country?** South Africa is a beautiful country, but we do have a problem with crime, so I would advise any travelers to do some research and make sure they go to safe areas and take care of their belongings while traveling.
- **What is a special holiday in your culture?** September 24 is Heritage Day in South Africa. On that day people from all cultures celebrate our unique heritage. Most people have a barbeque (which we call a braai), so we also call it Braai Day.
- **Are there any gestures or body language unique to your culture?** Most gestures from my culture are considered normal by Western standards. So, you can do thumbs up, thumbs down, middle finger (rude).
- **How has another culture influenced your own?** I have been living in South Korea for the past ten years and it has had a big impact on the way I interact with other people and see myself in this world.

1. **What are some common health practices?** Is homeopathy popular in your country? Homeopathy is almost like home medicine. Homeopathy, or Eastern medicine, is a different way of taking care of your body, like doing acupuncture for example.
2. **What thing from your culture do you wish the rest of the world would adopt (do)?** In general, South Africans are very friendly and sociable people. It's a kind of mindset of trying to make friends from all around the world. I wish the rest of the world would take on is this approach of connecting with other cultures.

38 Wishes

QUESTIONS & ANSWERS STUDENT A

1. **If you had one wish, what would you wish for?** I would wish for world peace so that everybody can live together in harmony. Not only stop all wars, but also end world hunger and environmental problems.
2. **Do you wish you were taller?** I am happy with how tall I am but I guess that most people wish they were taller.
3. **Can you remember what three wishes Aladdin wished for in the Disney movie?** Aladdin's first wish was to get out of the secret cave; second, to be a prince and the final wish was for the Genie to be free.
4. **Have any of your wishes ever come true?** Sometimes, if we're lucky, wishes do come true. For example, I wished to get a job at a university and eventually, after hard work and a little luck, my wish came true.
5. **What do you wish you could do after class?** I wish that after class I could go and spend the day at the beach. I want to swim, play on the sand, drink a cola and enjoy the warmth of summer.
6. **What do your parents wish for you?** My parents wish for me to be happy and successful. I guess right now they are praying for me to find a wife and start a family.
7. **What is the difference between goals and wishes?** Goals are wishes that you plan for. A wish is just something you want; a goal is something that you want and actively work to achieve.
8. **What do you wish would happen in your country?** I wish my country was run better so that there could be more businesses and more jobs so that people can be happier.
9. **What do you wish to be remembered for?** I hope to make a change in the future by helping teachers. I would do that with my YouTube channel or writing books. I hope to be remembered as someone who helped to improve education.
10. **Would you be happy if all your wishes came true?** Yes, I think I would be happy if all my wishes became true. Sometimes we wish for something and when it comes true, we regret it. But not in my case.

Q&A 38 WISHES STUDENT B

1. **What do you wish would happen today?** I hope to get all the work I need to accomplish done today. I also want to talk to everyone I love – that would be a good day!
2. **What would your best friend wish for?** I think my best friend would wish for a lot of money to enjoy life with. They want to have the freedom to live and do anything they want.
3. **When you were young, what did you wish to become?** I was never really sure of what I wanted to be when I was young. Eventually I became a teacher, and I am happy with my career.
4. **When do people make wishes in your culture?** You make a wish when you see a shooting star or when you blow out the candles on your birthday cake. Don't tell anyone what you wished for, otherwise it won't come true.
5. **What do you wish you could eat right now?** Actually, I'm a bit full at the moment. But perhaps some dessert or ice-cream would be nice.
6. **Do you wish you could travel back in time?** Yes, I think it would be interesting going back in time and seeing how people lived back then and compare it to modern life.
7. **How have your wishes changed compared to when you were young?** When I was young, my wishes had to do with the future; that I become rich, handsome and successful. Now my wishes focus on the present: I hope something good happens to me today.
8. **Do you wish you were born in another country?** I love being South African, but sometimes I wonder what my life would have been like if I was born in another country like Australia or America.
9. **What do you wish to achieve this year?** This year I wish to write a few books, shoot a video series that I can release and connect with many other people. Hopefully, if Covid-19 clears up, I would also like to travel somewhere.
10. **What do you wish to happen in the future?** Personally, I wish to reach 100,000 subscribers on my YouTube channel and also write a book to help teachers.

39 Gossip

QUESTIONS & ANSWERS STUDENT A

1. **What is gossip?** Gossip is when people talk about someone else's life; events in their lives or things they've done. People gossip because we are curious about each other, but gossip isn't good.

2. **Where do people usually gossip?** Gossip takes place where people chat. It can be during lunch breaks, in private or when you meet at the water cooler.

3. **Are you interested in celebrity gossip?** It is only human to be curious about celebrities; we wonder what is going on in their lives. Personally, I am not too interested in celebrities' lives.

4. **What are the most common topics for gossip?** Gossip usually involves someone's love life, some things they have done or problems they have in their lives. Gossip is almost always negative.

5. **What is the difference between gossip and a rumor?** Gossip is when you talk about somebody else behind their back and a rumor is a story that hasn't been proven true yet.

6. **Have you ever gotten someone in trouble by gossiping about them?** No, but I got into trouble because friends found out that I gossiped about them. So, to avoid getting into trouble, don't gossip.

7. **Do you think women gossip more than men?** I think both men and women gossip, but people believe that women gossip more.

8. **How would you deal with gossip about you?** If gossip is damaging to my career or people's perception about me, I will challenge them on it, otherwise they will continue to spread false rumors.

9. **After answering these questions about gossip, has your attitude towards it changed?** Yes, in future I will try to say only positive things about other people, although often gossip happens without thinking about it.

10. **Eleanor Roosevelt said: "Great minds discuss ideas; average minds discuss events; small minds discuss people." Do you agree?** If we look at society, great minds talk about ideas and how to improve the world.

Normal people talk about events in their lives and small-minded people discuss other people.

Q&A 39 GOSSIP STUDENT B

1. **Why do people enjoy gossip?** It is natural to gossip about other people, especially if it's juicy gossip. We like to talk about other people, especially if it is a bit negative. It's fun to share personal information about someone else.
2. **What is some gossip that you've recently heard?** My social group consists mainly of teachers so most gossip is about things that happen at school.
3. **Have you ever been the victim of gossip?** Yes, it was very negative and hurtful. In the future I will stay away from toxic people who gossip about me.
4. **What problems or pain can gossip cause?** When you gossip about someone else it could have a negative effect on their career or on their personal life. We should avoid gossip if possible.
5. **Have you ever gotten into trouble for gossiping?** I don't follow celebrity gossip too much, but it's usually about celebrity relationships.
6. **How would high school have been different if there was no gossip?** Gossip is the starting point of a lot of conflict in high school. Students spread rumors that can cause a lot of conflict. High school would be a much happier place for everyone if there was no gossip.
7. **How quickly does gossip spread in your school/workplace?** Because of social media gossip spreads even quicker. We should be cautious about what personal information gets on the internet.
8. **Can you trust a friend that likes to gossip?** Definitely not. Be careful with what information you share with them.
9. **If you heard some harmful gossip about someone you knew, what would you do?** If it is harmful gossip, I would ask the person gossiping not to continue sharing it with other people.
10. **"People are quick to believe bad things they hear about good people." Do you think this is true?** Definitely! It is a lot more interesting believing bad things than hearing good things. Bad news sells, that's human nature.

40 Birthday

QUESTIONS & ANSWERS STUDENT A

- **When is your birthday?** My birthday is March 18th.
- **What is the best gift you've ever received for your birthday?** The best gift I 've received for my birthday was a watch.
- **Do you ever read horoscopes? Do you believe in astrology?** No, I don't read horoscopes. Astrology is believing that the stars and your birthday have an effect on your personality and future.
- **Whose birthday do you always remember besides your own?** I always remember my parents' birthdays, because it is so important. I try to call them or give them a gift whenever it is their birthday.
- **Have you ever been to a surprise party?** Yes, when it was my dad's 40th birthday, my mom held a special surprise birthday party for him. She invited many family members and friends to surprise him.
- **What are some birthday traditions from your country?** Birthday traditions include eating cake, blowing out the candles, making a wish and receiving presents.
- **What are some significant birthdays by age?** Important birthdays include when your turn one in Korean culture, 13 in Jewish culture, Sweet 16, 18 and 21 because you are recognized as an adult, 50, 80 and 100.
- **What kind of cake would you like for your birthday?** (Design and flavor) I would like a big, carrot cake shaped like a rocket!
- **What do you do for your parents on their birthdays?** If I'm with my parents, I will give them a gift. If I can't meet them I will videocall them to wish dad or mom a happy birthday.
- **Among your friends and relatives, whose birthday is coming up next?** My mom's birthday was yesterday, February 20th so the next birthday is my dad's; March 10th.

Q&A 40 BIRTHDAY STUDENT B

- **How do you usually celebrate your birthday?** I like to celebrate my birthday by going out with friends and having a good time together. We get cake, have some drinks and celebrate together.

- **What present would you like for your next birthday?** For my next birthday I would like some cologne, to smell good.
- **What is your star sign?** My star sign is Pisces, the fish. What that means is that I was born under the constellation of Pisces.
- **What special days fall around your birthday?** The day before my birthday is Saint Patrick's Day, an Irish holiday.
- **How did you celebrate your birthday when you were young?** Yes, my parents always held a party for me. We would eat snacks and play games together.
- **What are some birthday traditions from other countries?** In some countries it's popular to prank a friend on their birthday. It could be by pressing their face into cake or surprising them.
- **What do you think is the best age to have a birthday?** The younger you are, the more you enjoy birthdays. As you get older, you still like your birthday, but it is not nearly as important as when you are young.
- **What is the most memorable birthday party you've been to?** I guess the most memorable birthday I've been to was for my dad. It was a surprise party my mom organized with family and friends. She even invited a popular singer to perform.
- **Do you think adults like birthdays?** Yes, I believe everyone enjoys their birthday, but as you get older, it doesn't matter to you as much anymore. It's still fun and important though.
- **How would you like to celebrate your birthday in ten years' time?** I would like to celebrate my birthday in ten years' time with my family. We could have a nice meal and look back and other memories.

41 Advice

QUESTIONS & ANSWERS STUDENT A

- **What does it mean to "ask for advice"?** Asking advice means that you have a problem and need someone's opinion on what to do about it.
- **What problem do you need advice for right now?** The biggest problem I have is finding the right wife!
- **What is some good advice you've heard recently?** I read the following quote on Instagram: "Only in the scariest cave will you find your treasure." That means that if you really want something badly enough, then you have to face your fears to get that treasure.
- **What problems do people normally ask advice for?** One of the most popular topics for advice is relationship advice.
- **What advice would you give to someone who wants to study English?** I would tell them to make English part of their daily life. Everything in their lives should be geared towards learning English.
- **Do you search for advice online?** What are some reputable (believable) sources? When I have a problem, I do a Google search for it. I use words like 'how to' or input my symptoms if I feel sick.
- **What advice would you give yourself when you were younger?** I would tell myself to be brave. There were many things that I wanted when I was young, but was too afraid to go for it. Even if I don't achieve my goal, the pursuit alone would improve me as a person.
- **What advice will you give if I say I want to quit smoking?** You should read a book called *'How to quit smoking'* by Alan Carr. In that book he gives lots of good tips and information on how to quit smoking.
- **What does it mean if I say don't listen to criticism if you won't want advice?** What does this mean? Criticism can be useful if it comes from a good source, but if it is only negative it won't help you.
- **What three pieces of advice would you give to your children or future children?** 'Be your best version of yourself and enjoy life. Become the best at something you enjoy.'

Q&A 41 ADVICE STUDENT B

- **Why do we ask other people for advice?** A friend, parent, or teacher can give us good advice to see our problem clearer and help us understand what to do.
- **Who do you usually ask for advice?** I usually ask advice from my friends. They usually give me advice, or they help me to feel better about my situation.
- **Have you ever given someone the wrong advice?** Maybe, but I can't remember, Whenever I give my honest opinion, I hope that it will prove useful.
- **What advice would you give yourself right now?** I would tell myself to relax and focus on the work at hand; do not get distracted by other things happening in life.
- **What is some good financial advice?** You want to be smart with how you spend your money. Whatever extra money you save, you should intelligently invest.
- **Has a friend ever come to you for advice with their love life?** Some friends come to me for advice on their love-life. Usually, it involves a problem in their relationship, or how to meet someone special.
- **What advice would you give to the leader of your country (or principal)?** I would tell our principal to focus resources on online education The world has changed and more schools should be fully prepared for online education.
- **What advice would you give if I want to get in shape (lose weight). What should I do?** If you want to get into shape, you should eat less food and exercise more, because 80% of our weight depends on your diet, and 20% on exercise.
- **Whose advice would you never take?** I would never take the advice of someone I don't respect. If someone isn't doing very well financially, I won't ask them for financial advice.
- **What advice would you give your parents?** My parents have helped me so much in my life, I would tell them to relax and to do things that they enjoy.

42 Environment

QUESTIONS & ANSWERS STUDENT A

- **Do you worry about the environment?** Yes, I worry about the environment. We need to leave earth for the next generation so we should take care of it now.
- **What is global warming?** Global warming is Earth becoming hotter. Because of air pollution the atmosphere is being damaged, trapping heat from the sun in earth's atmosphere, causing to planet to get warmer.
- **How can we solve littering?** Littering is when a person throws garbage outside. People should be taught from childhood how to recycle and throw away their trash instead of littering.
- **What can families do to help the environment?** Families should recycle and limit the amount of waste they create. When shopping they can take a reusable container instead of plastic bags.
- **What environmental problems are caused by transportation?** Most cars run on gas which creates air pollution. Fortunately, many companies are developing electric cars, which are better for the environment. People should also use different forms of transportation; like buses, trains, or bicycles.
- **What pollution bothers you the most?** The pollution that bothers me the most is water pollution. We often see rivers filled with trash or chemicals; it kills the fish and unsafe for humans to drink.
- **What will happen to the environment if pollution continues?** If we keep polluting the earth, we will destroy it 'beyond repair', which means that we will eventually die out with it. To preserve humanity, we should take care of the earth.
- **What's happening to the forests in the world?** Forests are shrinking because humans cut down millions of trees every year. Animals are dying because their habitats are shrinking. Humanity needs to protect our forests and trees.
- **Which countries are most responsible for pollution?** Countries with larger populations and more factories cause more pollution. That includes

India and China but it doesn't mean that the rest of the world can only blame them and not take responsibility for their own pollution.

10. **Renewable energy can help reduce pollution. Can you give examples of green energy?** Renewable energy has an unlimited supply and is safe to use, compared to gas which is limited and will eventually run out. Examples of green energy is solar energy, wind energy and thermal energy. Eventually we need to find a way to rely solely on renewable energy.

Q&A 42 ENVIRONMENT STUDENT B

1. **What environmental problems do we have right now?** The most alarming environmental problems have to do with the pollution either through trash in the ocean, or air pollution that we create through factories and car emissions.
2. **Why is climate change bad?** If the earth heats up, the polar ice caps will melt, which would cause the oceans' water levels to rise and that will have a devastating effect on the land.
3. **How do we recycle?** We recycle by placing trash in pre-determined areas to be reused. Recyclable materials include cans, glass, paper and other plastics.
4. **How can stop companies from polluting too much?** It is the duty of governments to restrict the amount of pollution that companies create. They do this by imposing fines if a companies' output of pollution is higher than normal. As individuals we can boycott companies by not buying their products.
5. **What problems are caused by technology?** The process of making new technological products can cause pollution. Because of the increase of technology, there is also an increased need for energy. The creation of this energy causes pollution.
6. **The earth is 70% water. Are you worried about water pollution?** Yes, I'm very worried about water pollution. We often see photos or videos of trash in the ocean, rivers and lakes. Chemical or oils spills kill animals, poisons the water and leaves it unusable for humans. We really need to take care of our water supply.
7. **What causes air pollution?** When factories release chemicals into the air

it causes air pollution. Motor vehicles and livestock release gas that is damaging to earth's atmosphere.

3. **How will the world look in 100 years?** In a hundred years the world will be less polluted due to new energy sources and people will be better educated on taking care of the environment.

4. **How can countries work together to save the earth?** Countries should work together to save the earth. They need to co-operate and enforce rules that stop excess pollution. They could have incentives to help smaller countries from not creating as much trash and pollution.

5. **What are some downsides to using renewable energy sources?** The problem with renewable energy resources such as solar and wind energy is that it is not as efficient as burning coal or gas. We would need to change our priorities, such as using more renewable energy and on preserving earth's resources.

43 Family

QUESTIONS & ANSWERS STUDENT A

1. **How many people are there in your family?** In my family we are six people: My mom and dad, older brother, me and two younger brothers.
2. **What is something you like about your mom or dad?** Of course, everybody loves their mom and dad. I really appreciate my mom taking care of us; she is an amazing cook, very sensitive and caring. My dad is very hard working.
3. Are your parents strict? When I was young my parents were very strict, because they had four boys! But as I grew older my parents relaxed and became more lenient.
4. What is something that your family does together? My family usually watches sport, eat dinner or lunch and also pray together.
5. Who does the cooking at home? Right now, I live alone, so unfortunately, I do the cooking. But when I'm with my family, my mom does all the cooking and we do the dishes after.
6. Do you ever wish to get away from your family? Yes, from an early age I started moving away from my family to go study and to work in another country. But I always love and miss my family. So, it feels good to be re-united and spend time together.
7. Do you have a large, extended family? Yes, we are very close to my mother's side of the family and my dad' side. On my dad's side, he has many sisters, so we have many cousins; on my mom's side she has a brother and a couple of sisters. Therefore, I have a very large extended family.
8. How are families changing compared to the past? In the past, families used to be quite large, with four, five, six or maybe more children being born. These days people are planning their families and having fewer kids.
9. Would you like to start a family in the future? Yes, my plan is to get married in the future and start a family, but I'm running out of time, so I'll have start fairly soon.
10. What is the most valuable lesson your parents taught you? My parents

have taught me the value of working hard and setting goals for the future. That's the only way to reach success; by working hard and following your dreams.

Q&A 43 FAMILY STUDENT B

1. **How old is everyone in your family?** Well, I hope my family does not mind, but my dad is I think 64, my mom 59, my older brother is turning 38, I am 35, my younger brother is 33 and my youngest brother is 27.
2. **Do you get along with your siblings?** Siblings are brothers or sisters. When we were younger, we used to get into a lot of fights, but whenever we are together right now, we get along. Even though our personalities are very different, we understand each other.
3. **What are some rules that your parents have?** The main rule my parents had was don't break anything, don't hurt your brothers and clean after yourself.
4. **How does your family celebrate holidays?** On vacations we would go to the beach; for shorter holidays we relax at home and play sports outside. For big events like Christmas, we prepare a big meal at home.
5. **What chores do you do at home?** When my brothers and I were young, we hung up the laundry, did the dishes or tidied our rooms. We also helped our dad in the garden by raking leaves or moving the lawn.
6. **What do you wish you could change about your family?** I wish we were living close to each other with good jobs in a safe and prosperous country.
7. **How often do you meet your extended family?** In the past we used to meet around Christmas time, so once a year. But right now, I live in South Korea, which is very far away, so I only get to meet them every couple of years.
8. **Why do some people choose not to get married or to have children?** The main reason for people not getting married is lack of money. It is very expensive to get married and start a family. The other reason is that people want to enjoy their lives, instead of settling down.
9. **What is your ideal partner or family?** My ideal partner is someone that I with similar value, caring and family-orientated.
10. **What will you teach your children in the future?** Obviously, I want to

raise my future children to be capable adults and to enjoy their lives. I also want to instill confidence in them to chase their dreams and achieve the success they want in their lives.

44 Social Media

QUESTIONS & ANSWERS STUDENT A

- **What social media apps to you have on your phone?** On my phone I have many social media apps, but the main ones are Facebook, Instagram and also Kakao Talk, a popular South Korean messenger.
- **Do you post content or only view other people online?** The majority of people online are called lurkers. A lurker is someone who only views other people's social media, but they don't often post anything of their own. For myself, I often post to social media. My preferred media to post on is Instagram and Facebook.
- **What is your favorite channel on YouTube?** Besides my YouTube channel, Etacude, I also enjoy watching some sports and pop culture channels. The last video I watched was about 'How to grow your YouTube audience'.
- **What content do you watch on Instagram or Facebook?** My social media is mainly for family and friends. I do follow some success and quote pages on Instagram, but the majority of people that I follow, are people that I know.
- **Which creators do you think are overrated?** There are too many people creating gaming content and the market is very saturated, which means that there are too creators in the same niche.
- **What are the positives of using social media?** There was no social media when I was young so I rarely took any photos. Now I'm creating a visual memory of what I do every week. I enjoy posting on social media because it allows me connect with my family and friends.
- **Do you think the new generation is better at using social media?** Young people have grown up in this new age of social media, so they are savvy in terms of what to put on the internet. I believe it to be a blessing and a curse to have grown up with phones. A blessing because of the new opportunities it has created, and a curse because they can't be without their phones.
- **How can social media be used to improve your career?** Yes, social

media can be used to improve your career. In the past it was difficult to display your skills and life publicly, but now, thanks to social media, employers can see what you have to offer. Just be careful not to share any material that might display you in a negative way.

- **Do you think social media will change in the future?** How will it evolve? I believe that social media use will increase in the future as people get more used to it. Young people these days understand the power of influence online, where you are connected to millions of people.
- **Social media is very addictive. How can we protect ourselves from using it too much?** Media addiction is a major problem with younger people, because we have FOMO - fear of missing out. It is important to have some time away from technology to enjoy life naturally.

Q&A - 44 SOCIAL MEDIA - STUDENT B

- **Can you list the most popular social networking apps?** The most popular social media apps are Facebook, Instagram, Twitter and LinkedIn. Some countries have their own social networking apps.
- **How often do you post on social media?** I use social media frequently. I post perhaps once every day on different apps; this is necessary for me as I have a YouTube channel.
- **What is the last video you watched on YouTube?** I really love watching documentary videos. The last video I've watched was a National Geographic documentary on penguins.
- **Do you follow your friends on Instagram or Facebook?** Who posts the most? Yes, I follow my friends on Instagram and Facebook. In general, the demographic group that posts the most are women between 20 and 30.
- **Which creators do you really like and why?** I really enjoy YouTube creators like Brian G and Roberto Blake, as they give tips and advice to help YouTubers.
- **What are the negatives of social media?** We use social media to connect with other people, which could be dangerous; You can get scammed; your information could be stolen and used by criminals. So, you have to be cautious when using social media.
- **What can older people learn from the youth about social media?** Young people understand the power of the internet and social media. Its

influence has the power to control people's thoughts.

7. **How can you use social media to display your life?** You can share pictures or short videos of interesting things in your life, celebrate achievements or show off skills on Instagram or Facebook.

8. **What rules should parents give their children about using social media?** The first rule that we should give our kids is not to share their personal information or photos of themselves with strangers; and to limit the amount of time that they use their phones, because it's easy to get addicted to social media.

9. **If you could remove any social media app, which one would it be?** If I could get rid of any social media app, it would be Snapchat, since most other social media apps now can also add filters.

45 Animals

QUESTIONS & ANSWERS STUDENT A

- **What is your favorite animal?** My favorite animal is a dog, but my favorite wild animal is an elephant.
- **What animal most represents your character?** I would like the think that my character is something like a jaguar, but it's probably more like a beaver – obsessed with working towards a goal.
- **What animals are there in your country?** I am originally from South Africa and we have many wild animals. The most well-known animals in Africa are called the big five: The elephant, lion, buffalo, rhino and leopard.
- **If you could have a pet animal, what would it be?** I would like something exotic, but not too dangerous. Perhaps something like a buffalo, that I can train and ride.
- **What animals do we eat?** Humans have been raising animals for consumption for thousands of years. Consumption means to eat or take in. The main animals we eat are chickens, pigs, cattle (cows) and sheep. Millions of these animals are raised for food, but that requires a lot of resources like water and grass. We should try to eat less meat in the future.
- **Is it okay to use animals for sport?** Yes, horses enjoy running and so do greyhounds. Sheepherding dogs love their work. But bull-fighting, as well as illegal dog and cockerel fighting are cruel events that must be outlawed.
- **Do you know any animals that have gone extinct?** One of the most famous animals that has gone extinct in the last few hundred years (1681) has been the dodo; a big bird on the island of Mauritius.
- **How can we save animals from going extinct?** Animals need a safe place to live, so we have to protect national parks. The land and the forests are shrinking, so we have to create safe areas where animals can live freely without being poached.
- **Should animals be bred?** Yes, if we want certain species to survive, we have to help them breed. In most cases it is our fault for killing off so many animals that they end up endangered.

). **How have animals evolved to survive?** It's very interesting how some animals survive. Some monkeys, for example, move to urban areas and steal from humans to survive. Many birds flock to city centers to get food more easily.

ANSWERS Q45 ANIMALS STUDENT B

- **Do you have any pets?** Right now, I don't have any pets but I would love to get a dog of my own to raise.
- **What animal ability would you like to have?** Most people would probably say that they would like to fly, but I would prefer having a keen sense of hearing. That way I could get more information from my surroundings.
- **What are some national animals from other countries?** America is known for the bald eagle, South Korea for the white tiger, South Africa for the springbok antelope, Russia has bears, France's animal is a rooster, Australia is known for its kangaroos and China for its panda bears.
- **What animal are you afraid of?** I'm afraid of snakes. I don't like touching or going near snakes. I understand however that they are important for the eco-system so they should be protected.
- **How do we use animals except for eating?** We use pets like cats and dogs for companionship; dogs also sniff out explosions and drugs, and animals like donkeys can pull heavy loads on farms.
- **Is it okay to use animals for testing products?** I would say no, there must be better ways to test products. Only in lifesaving circumstances should animal testing be done.
- **How are humans dangerous to animals?** Humans are the greatest threat to animals, because we destroy their habitats and kill them for our own needs. People who kill animals illegally are called poachers, who try to make money from endangered animals such as rhinos for their horns.
- **Should animals be kept in zoos?** Some animals need to be in zoos where they can be bred to increase their numbers. They can also be used for people to learn from but it is still sad to see animals in cages. We need more parks and nature reserves where animals can live normal lives.
- **How do you feel about hunting?** In many cases hunting is necessary. Hunters pay a lot of money to hunt animals which is used to support the

game reserves. When there are too many of a certain species, hunting regulates the number of animals.

10. **Where is the best place in the world to see animals?** Africa has some of the most fascinating animals on earth so I would suggest visiting a country in Southern Africa.

46 Learning English

QUESTIONS & ANSWERS STUDENT A

- **How many languages do you speak?** I speak two languages, English and Afrikaans. I'm also studying Korean.
- **What are the four language skills and which one is most difficult for you?** The four languages skills are: Speaking, listening, reading and writing. The most difficult skill for most people is speaking, because it is something that you have to practice out loud.
- **When you travel to a new country, what are some key expressions to learn?** When I travel to another country I usually learn 'hello', 'thank you', 'how much is it', 'where is the bathroom' and 'goodbye'.
- **How can you use the internet to learn English?** The internet is a fantastic resource and we can find all kinds of information for learning a language. There are videos on YouTube, online courses and you can even connect with online teachers.
- **Who was your favorite English teacher and how did they help you?** My best English teacher helped me become more confident by organizing speaking activities in class.
- **How do you practice speaking English?** I practice English by speaking with my friends. Sometimes I join a study group where we practice speaking together about different topics.
- **Who is the best English speaker among your friends and family?** I have very smart friends who speak English very fluently. I try to become a better speaker by imitating him.
- **What kind of attitude is important when learning a new language?** When learning a new language, you should not be embarrassed to speak out loud. If you never practice the language, you will never improve.
- **Have you had an embarrassing experience when speaking English?** It is difficult using a second language in front of many people. I have had some embarrassing situations where I made a mistake in front of a large audience.
- **Translators are rapidly improving. Do you think people will ever stop**

learning languages? No, even though translators are getting better, I don't think people will stop learning languages. Learning a new skill improves brain function and gives a valuable asset for the future.

Q&A - 46 LEARNING ENGLISH - STUDENT B

- **When did you start studying English?** I've studied English since I was very young and learned how to read and write at school.
- **Why do you study English?** I study English to improve my job prospects. The world is getting more connected therefore people are learning English to communicate globally.
- **What important words do beginners need to learn first?** Beginners should focus on learning the alphabet and then basic sight words. Sight words are the most useful words that beginners need to know.
- **Do you watch TV to learn English and which shows do you enjoy?** Many people have learned English by watching the American TV sitcom, 'Friends'. It is still popular because the characters use common phrases and their pronunciation and speed of speaking is easy to understand.
- **How do you learn new vocabulary?** Vocabulary opens the door to a new language; start by learning useful words and phrases in context. Expand your knowledge by practicing synonyms, antonyms and exceptions.
- **What are some similar words between your language and English?** There are many English loan words – taxi, TV, drama. Internet and technological words that commonly also appear in other languages.
- **Why do people get embarrassed when they speak English?** When you learn a new skill it's okay to make mistakes, because the more English you use, the faster you will improve.
- **Have you ever studied with a tutor?** It was good working with a tutor one-on-one, they fixed my mistakes and helped me improve. I got all the attention and they taught me new words, phrases and grammar.
- **What was your best English-speaking experience?** When traveling, I always try to speak to native English speakers and listen to their accents. If you get a chance and meet an English native speaker, have a short conversation with them, it's a good English-speaking experience to have.
- **How would you teach someone your native language?** First, I would

teach them all the most important and used words. Then I will teach them common expressions so that they can start using the language as soon as possible.

47 Last Time

QUESTIONS & ANSWERS STUDENT A

- **When is the last time you went shopping?** I went shopping this afternoon. I bought some vegetables and chicken to cook for dinner.
- **When is the last time you cried?** A couple of weeks ago I watched a very sad movie and cried a little bit. It was a good movie, but it made me feel very sad.
- **When is the last time you did any chores?** I usually do chores at home a couple of times a week. Yesterday I swept the floor and washed the dishes. Tomorrow I have to do the laundry and dust the windows.
- **When is the last time someone shouted at you?** A few weeks ago, I forgot my wallet at a convenience store. As I left, the store clerk ran after me and shouted: "Hey, you forgot your wallet!" Usually, people shout at you when they are angry, in this case she shouted at me to get my attention.
- **When is the last time you said sorry?** We apologize and say that we are sorry when we did something wrong. The last time I have apologized was when I made a mistake with my students. I corrected a mistake and said "sorry".
- **When is the last time you ran into an old friend?** A few days ago, I ran into a colleague; I was surprised to meet him and we had a short conversation before parting ways.
- **When is the last time you had a problem with your computer?** Last week the word processor on my computer didn't work. So, I contacted a computer repairman who fixed it for me remotely. Even though he lived far away, he connected to my computer and fixed the problem.
- **When is the last time you laughed out loud?** Every night before bed, I look at some funny pictures. Last night I saw a very funny meme and I laughed out loud.
- **When is the last time you felt amazing?** Last week I went to the gym and I had a really good work-out session. Afterwards, I took a shower and felt absolutely amazing.

*   **When is the last time you received a gift?** I went to visit a friend of mine in another city; she gave me a bottle of wine as a present. That was the last time I received a gift.

Q&A - 47 LAST TIME - STUDENT B

*   **When is the last time you said no?** At my workplace you can choose to do extra work and for extra pay. I was asked if I wanted to do extra work but I declined - I said no. Right now, I have other things that I want to do with my time.
*   **When is the last time you went to the cinema?** Before lock down started, I went to the cinema. I saw a war movie and was the only person in the theatre!
*   **When is the last time you were late?** I really hate being late, but the last time I was late some friends were waiting for me. I got stuck doing something else and I was a couple of minutes late.
*   **When is the last time someone did something nice for you?** I left my bag at a friend's house. Today, he brought my bag all the way from his home and gave it to me. That was a really kind gesture.
*   **When is the last time you were lost?** A couple of weeks ago, I was walking around an area I didn't know very well. I got lost walking around the buildings, but eventually found my way home.
*   **When is the last time you traveled by train?** Last week I took the train from my hometown to the capital city, Seoul. It took about two and a half hours. I really enjoy traveling by train.
*   **When is the last time you did your homework?** I haven't done homework for a long time, but I always prepare to teach my classes in advance. It is always smart to be prepared for the future.
*   **When is the last time you had a haircut?** The last time I had a haircut was a couple of months ago. Very soon, I will have to go to the hair salon to get a new haircut.
*   **When is the last time you went dancing?** These days it is not safe to go dancing in big groups, but last year I met some friends and we went dancing for Halloween.
*   **When is the last time you helped a friend?** I helped a friend of mine

move to a new apartment a few weeks ago. It was hard work, but that's what friends are for.

48 How do you?

QUESTIONS & ANSWERS STUDENT A

- **How do you make ice?** To make ice, pour water into an ice-tray, then put it in the freezer. After some time, it will turn into ice.
- **How do you fall asleep easily?** To fall asleep easily, don't eat two hours before going to bed. Avoid electronic devices an hour before going to bed – rather read a book. Turn off all lights. In bed, relax your body and the muscles in your face; breathe deeply and imagine yourself somewhere peaceful, like in a canoe drifting on a lake.
- **How do you make someone fall in love with you?** Like the genie in Aladdin says, you can't make someone fall in love with you, but you can take care of yourself and practice your social skills. Try to get to know the person, show them your personality and have fun.
- **How do you take care of your skin?** Every morning and night I wash my face and apply toner. When the toner dries, I apply face lotion. Start taking care of your skin from an early age.
- **How do you give a good presentation?** A good presentation depends all on how you engage the audience. Smile, ask them questions and tell stories. Make good eye-contact and use confident body language.
- **How do you climb a mountain?** You climb a mountain one step at a time! You need the right equipment and shoes. Plan how long it will take to reach the peak, then hike the mountain at a steady pace. Remember to take breaks and hydrate by drinking water.
- **How do you control your anger?** To control your anger, you have to separate your ego from the source of anger. Don't internalize the reason for your anger, take a deep breath and think about how you can resolve the problem.
- **How do you make a burger?** To make a burger you need a hamburger bun, beef patty, some lettuce, tomato, onion and cheese. First cut open the bun and slice the onion and tomato. Grill the patty in a pan. Now add the lettuce, tomato and onion in the bun. Place the patty on top, add cheese and some ketchup to finish your hamburger.

9. **How do you study for an exam?** First, I separate the work I need to study into units; I focus on important material likely to be in the test. I then study, review and repeatedly go through the work. I relax and rest the night before the exam.
10. **How do you enjoy a day at the beach?** I love going to the beach. I take a towel, parasol, sunglasses, and sunblock with me. At the beach, I apply some sunblock and lie on my towel. When I get too hot, I go and swim in the waves.

Q&A - 48 HOW DO YOU? - STUDENT B

1. **How do you wash the dishes?** Before I wash the dishes, I rinse it and clean the sink. Then I use a dishwash liquid to scrub the plates and leave them to dry.
2. **How do you lose weight?** Losing weight is eighty percent diet. So, in order to lose weight, you need to eat less food in smaller portions and avoid foods with flour and sugar.
3. **How do you quit smoking?** Smoking is not difficult to quit, you just need to make up your mind and understand that you have brainwashed yourself to think that you need cigarettes. So, when you understand that, quit. Don't reduce smoking. Resist the craving and it will go away in five minutes. If you don't smoke for two weeks, you are almost cured.
4. **How do you take a good photo?** To take a good photo, make sure that the person is in frame, also that there is good lighting on them. Take out any distracting things and keep it simple. Ask them to have a good posture, smile or to have a nice pose. Take many photos to find the best one possible.
5. **How do you play table tennis?** There are two ways to hold a table tennis racket, the 'shake hand' and 'pen-holder' grips. Play against a wall or practice with a friend. Table tennis is a lot of fun.
6. **How do you make new friends?** To make a good friend, try to find things that you have in common, maybe similar hobbies or interests, or just being in the same social group. Treat them well and invite them to events so that you can get to know each other.

7. **How do you stop hiccups?** I stop hiccups by relaxing. Some people drink water or hold their breaths, but I slowly breathe in and out and relax my body. Eventually the hiccups will end.
8. **How do you take care of a puppy?** A puppy needs lots of care and attention; from potty-training, to teaching it to sleep in its own sleeping crate; feeding, training and exercising it.
9. **How do you plan a party?** To have a party, you need a venue, people, things to do and eat. Do you need music and decorations? Send invitations and remember to tell them what to wear and bring. Think about who will clean up after the party.
10. **How do you become rich?** To become rich, you need a high paying job; or you need to save a lot of money and then invest it; or you can start some kind of business or sell a product. By just having a normal job it will be very difficult. You need to find other income streams, not just your salary, to become wealthy.

49 What if?

QUESTIONS & ANSWERS STUDENT A

- **What if you only had 24 hours left to live, what would you do?** If I only had 24 hours left to live, I would spend that time with my friends and family before I pass away.
- **If you could date any celebrity, who would it be?** If I could date any celebrity, it would be Blake Lively. She is beautiful and we share similar hobbies. Unfortunately, she is already married so that would never happen.
- **If you could do any job, what would it be?** Right now, I really enjoy my job at the university as an English lecturer. It gives me the opportunity to be creative and help my students.
- **If you were world famous, what would it be for?** If I was world famous, I would want it to be because I helped humanity in some way; not for sports or entertainment.
- **If you could solve any problem in the world, what would it be?** If I could solve any problem, I would like to help teachers be better inside the classroom, because that will also help their students. That is my goal for the future.
- **If you could change one thing about yourself, what would it be?** If I could change only one thing about myself, I would change the way that I overthink things and procrastinate.
- **If you could see into the future to find out one thing, what would you like to know?** I would like to know when the world would get back to normal; when we can travel, meet our friends and socialize without worrying about being in groups.
- **If an alien came to Earth, what would you show it?** I would take an alien to a school to show it the energy and the joy that children have. The alien would see all the goodness and happiness that is possible on Earth.
- **If you didn't need to sleep, what would you do with your nights?** I would like to learn new skills and improve myself as much as possible. But some of the time I would relax by watching movies and playing

computer games.

10. **If you could stop a bad habit that you have, which habit would it be?** A bad habit that I have is that I bite my nails. It's not because I'm nervous, but it is a habit I need to get rid of.

Q&A - 49 WHAT IF? - STUDENT B

1. **If you were a toy, what toy would you want to be?** If I was a toy, I would like to be a go-kart, because go-karts are fast, noisy and people really enjoy driving them.
2. **If you could go anywhere for a holiday, where would you go?** These days I would like to go and visit countries around the Mediterranean Sea; eat great food, enjoy nice weather and spend my time near the beach.
3. **If you had a million dollars, what would you buy?** If I had a million dollars, I would buy property that I could rent out and perhaps invest the rest.
4. **If you were a sculptor artist, what object would you sculpt?** The greatest artists are the ones that sculpt the human body, because it is so difficult and intricate. So, if I could sculpt anything, it would be the human body, especially like Michelangelo or Leonardo da Vinci.
5. **If you could have invented one thing, what thing would it have been?** If I could have invented anything, it would be the light bulb. The use of electric light has allowed civilization to evolve more rapidly.
6. **If you had any superpower, what would it be?** If I could have any superpower, I would like to be telekinetic - which means that I can move objects with my mind.
7. **If you could be a character in any movie, who would it be?** If I could be a character from a movie, it probably would be Ironman. He has a big company and use those resources to invent new technology to help humanity.
8. **If you could start and run a business, what kind of business would it be?** If I could start any business, it will be something online, products that I can create digitally. It would be to help people with products or information to improve their lives.
9. **If you could re-live your life from the start, how would you live it**

differently? Now that I understand the world better than I did when I was young, I would make smarter decisions and devote my time to different skills. I would learn about investing, because it is important to start when you are young.

9. **If you were the best in the world at something, what would it be?** If I were the best teacher in the world, I would be able to teach things in a simple way and help more people. I'm not the best teacher in the world – but I would like to learn from other teachers so I can reach the peak of my potential.

50 Social Issues

QUESTIONS & ANSWERS STUDENT A

- **Does your country have a problem with pollution?** I'm living in South Korea and although the country doesn't have a problem with waste and water pollution, there is definitely a problem with air pollution.
- **What problems does your city have?** I live in a city called Daegu where it gets very hot during summer. When it gets too hot everyone stays inside with air-conditioning.
- **How can we take care of the elderly?** We have to take care of our elderly. These days people are living longer because of improved health care, but that means they might not have the resources to take care of themselves. It is society's responsibility to care for it's old people.
- **What is the traditional role of men and women?** In the past men were seen as the breadwinners, they would work to get money, whereas women stayed at home and raised the kids. These days things are changing, we are more equal and each gender can decide on how they want to spend their lives.
- **Is there a population problem in your country?** Are there too many or too few people? South Korea has an aging population, which means that the elderly is getting much older and young people are not having many babies. This will cause problems in the future.
- **What is racism?** Racism is to treat someone unfairly based on the color of their skin. We are all expected to be treated equal based on who we are inside and our abilities, not on the color of our skin. Martin King Junior said that he had a dream of judging people on their character, not the color of their skin.
- **How is poverty and crime connected?** Poverty means that there is not enough money. People don't have jobs or they are not earning enough money to sustain themselves and they sometimes turn to a life of crime, so poverty creates more crime.
- **How has your country improved access for handicapped people?** Handicapped people have some kind of disability. On subways and in

elevators you will find some Braille (writing) so blind people can read it, and other places have access for wheelchairs.

- **Should racial minorities be given an advantage when applying for a job?** Affirmative action is to give priority, or an advantage, to someone of color and also to women above men. The reason for that is that they want multi-cultural and diverse people working together.
- **Do you believe all social issues can be solved?** No, unfortunately, there will always be problems. Even when technology improves or civilization advances, it creates new problems.

Q&A - 50 SOCIAL ISSUES - STUDENT B

- **Do you think cigarettes should be banned?** Personally, I think cigarettes should be banned. They cause so much illness around the world. Not only do they have a negative impact on a smoker's health, but because it is addictive, it also affects a smoker's mind.
- **Have you ever done any volunteering? If you haven't, what would you want to do?** Yes, a couple of years ago I volunteered to teach English at an orphanage. It was an intense experience where I could see some underprivileged kids and spent some time with them.
- **How can the government help homeless people?** Most people become homeless because of some big problem in their homes or a financial difficulty. Many of them also suffer from alcohol or drug addiction. The first thing the government can do is it can provide safe shelters for the homeless and opportunities to earn a living.
- **Is the modern workplace fair towards women?** More women are moving up into managerial positions but are still not represented in all careers. Jobs should be based on qualifications and abilities and not on gender.
- **Is crime a problem in your country and what kind crimes are committed?** I am originally from South Africa and crime is a massive problem due to unemployment and corruption. There are many hijackings (taking your car), burglaries and armed robberies.
- **How do you feel about abortion?** Abortion is a very difficult topic. Many people believe a woman has the right to her body, whereas people who are against abortion believe that the baby's life is valuable.

- **Is alcoholism or drugs a problem in your country?** Drugs isn't a problem in Korea because they are very strict on it. Alcoholism on the other hand is a problem because of peer pressure and social customs.
- **Why is it a bad thing if people come into your country illegally?** People that enter a country illegally could be criminals or bring other problems with them.
- **Are there enough jobs in your country? How can the government make more?** No, there are not nearly enough jobs for unskilled people. Most people prefer white-collar, high-paying jobs and ignoring jobs that require manual labor.
- **Less than 0.1% of people use sign language. Should every speech or public broadcast have someone using sign language?** Everybody deserves to be heard and to have access to information; but I'm not sure if it is necessary that every speech has to be translated into sign-language.

51 Personality

QUESTIONS & ANSWERS STUDENT A

- **Are you an introvert or an extrovert?** Introverted people are shy. People that prefer being alone and they get energy when they are by themselves. Extroverts are people that enjoy being social and get energy when they are with other people.
- **When you are angry, how do you calm yourself down?** I usually take a step back; I breathe and I ask myself: 'Why are you angry?' I try to put myself outside of the situation to calm down.
- **Can you describe your best friend's personality?** My best friend is cool and calm. We get along because we have similar interests and the same sense of humor.
- **What is your star sign? Do you believe in astrology?** Astrology is believing in star signs having an effect on your personality and future. My star sign is Pisces, or the fish. You also get the Chinese Zodiac which has a sign for every 12 years. I don't believe in astrology.
- **What is your best personality trait?** I am very social and positive. I try and be friendly and sociable.
- **What kind of personality does a good leader need?** A good leader needs to be smart, brave and above all, an independent thinker with wisdom in handling people and making good decisions.
- **Do you find it easy to make friends?** It is easy for me to talk to people, to get to know them and make acquaintances; but to become close friends there needs to be synergy between the two of you.
- **Who or what has shaped your personality?** Our experiences, our parents and our families shape our personalities. The way that we were brought up and the experiences we had will impact how our personalities are formed.
- **Is your personality suited to your future job?** In general, I believe that teachers should be friendly and easy to approach by their students.
- **'Nice guys finish last.' What does it mean and do you agree?** People that don't have a strong personality and fight for what they want, lose out

to those who are louder. Don't let other people push you around, be strong and go for your goals, but be a kind person in general.

Q&A - 51 PERSONALITY - STUDENT B

- **Who is your role model?** I've never had a role model; someone that I wanted to follow. So recently I heard somebody say that your role model should be you, ten years from now.
- **Are you shy? What situations give you anxiety?** No, I'm not shy. I like talking to people and don't mind speaking in front of a crowd. To get better at public speaking you should do it more, because the more you put yourself in uncomfortable situations, the more you will grow.
- **How would your friends describe you?** I believe my friends would say that I'm a friendly, sociable guy. It is easy for me to talk to someone, but I'm also stubborn.
- **What is your blood type? Do you think personality is linked to blood type?** My blood type is A +. Many people in Asia believe that your blood type influences your personality, but I don't think that is true.
- **If you could change one thing about your personality, what would it be?** I tend to overthink situations. After making a mistake, I regret and constantly think about it. I would like to change that part of my personality.
- **How has your personality changed over the years?** When I was young, I was kind of shy and made a lot of jokes. As I got older, I became more talkative and social. Now as I'm getting older, I feel like I'm becoming more reserved and relaxed.
- **Do you like personality tests? Have you ever done a Myers- Briggs test?** Yes, recently I did one of those personality tests. It is very interesting and you get to know something about yourself. I do not think they are one hundred percent accurate, but it is a fun way to think about yourself.
- **What is something that most people don't know about you?** Even though I seem very busy, I'm in a constant battle to overcome procrastination and do the work that I set out for myself to do. I'm always reading books and trying new techniques to get myself to take action.
- **What personality trait do you wish you had?** Even though I'm very social, I wish I was more confident. I tend to listen to what others say and

I can sometimes be easily persuaded.

9. **Do people fall in love with looks or personality?** People are attracted by looks; that is what gets you interested in another person. But what creates love is personality, connection and chemistry.

52 Job Interview

QUESTIONS & ANSWERS STUDENT A

- **Why should we hire you?** You should hire me not only because I have experience and good qualifications, but also because I am a passionate worker that always gives one hundred percent on whatever project I work on.
- **Please tell me about yourself, where did you grow up?** I was born in 1985 in a city called Bloemfontein in South Africa. But I grew up and went to university in another town called Potchefstroom.
- **What are your qualifications?** I have a Master Degree in Education. I also have various teaching certificates that I have done in order to become the best teacher possible.
- **What do you know about this company?** I am really interested in working for this company. I've looked at the history of this company, its products and goals for the future. I feel that I can contribute as a team player in this great company.
- **What are your biggest strengths?** I'm a very hard worker and I do my best to achieve my goals. I work well with others when doing projects and it's easy for me to stay focused on the job at hand.
- **Are you a good team player?** Yes, I am very professional in my communication with others. I also try to maintain a friendly work environment and help team members whenever they need assistance.
- **Are you good at handling difficult or stressful situations?** Give an example. I don't get stressed too easily and whenever I face a problem, I do my best to overcome it. I believe that stressful situations can be useful to get the best out of me, so I will do my best to overcome any difficulty that might arise.
- **What would you like to learn in this company?** I really want to gain experience in this company. I want to learn from my seniors and do my best to complete my assignments. While being here I hope to mature and improve my knowledge and my career.
- **How well does your personality fit this job?** I am a very goal driven and

social person. Whenever a task is given to me, I focus and do my best to achieve it. Also, I like working with other people, so this job will suit me very well.

10. **How do you handle conflict at work?** Tell me about how you handled a problem with a coworker or customer. At a previous job, I had a co-worker who disagreed with me, so we aired our grievances and what could have become a bad relationship was fixed.

Q&A - 52 JOB INTERVIEW - STUDENT B

- **Why do you want this job?** I believe that this job will be great for my career. I can gain a lot of experience and get to know other people that work in the same field as I do.
- **What do you consider your biggest achievement?** My greatest achievement is helping others. During my studies I have been able to work with other teachers and push them to achieve their goals. I've also done well in my studies, where I was one of the best students in class.
- **Do you have relevant work experience?** Yes, I have done similar work in the past. I have experience working with other people and I work hard to achieve the goals set by my previous job. I really want to learn even more by working at this company.
- **Where do you see yourself in 5 years?** In five-years' time I would love to be working at the company, but my responsibilities will have changed as I've gained experience. I hope to become a valuable part of this company and contribute to its success however I can.
- **What are your biggest weaknesses?** Sometimes I say yes too quickly. Whenever someone asks me to help on a project I agree, which could lead to me taking on too much work at one time.
- **What salary and benefits do you expect?** I hope to get a better than average salary so I can enjoy this job without worrying too much about my finances.
- **Are you a good leader? Can you give an example?** Yes, I believe that I have strong leadership potential. At my previous job I often lead teams on projects. I am good at delegating and getting the best out of people.
- **Why did you leave your last job?** Even though I enjoyed my last job, I believe that I need to come to this company to be challenged and achieve

greater things.

8. **What do you wish to accomplish in the first 90 days of this job?** In the first 90 days I would like to find my feet and get to know everyone I'll be working with. I would also want to create a good impression of myself so that my co-workers can see that I'm a valuable asset to the company.

9. **Do you have any questions for me?** Yes, what does the ideal candidate look like for this position? How can I improve my application?

Thank you for reading 1000 English Questions and Answers!